Sikhism

A Christian Approach

Marcus Braybrooke

Sikhism
A Christian Approach

The book was finished in mid-August 2017:
Seventy years from the Independence of India
and the Partition of the sub-continent,
which caused so many deaths
and so great suffering.
The book is dedicated to the memory of those who died with the
prayer that the great faiths
will teach us all to live together in harmony

ISBN 978-0-24-244-30699-1
First Edition

Braybrooke Press
17 Courtiers Green, OX14 3EN
www.marcusbraybrooke.com

www.lulu.com

CONTENTS

Sikhism

There is but One God
Eternal Truth is His Name
Creator of All Things
All-pervading Spirit
Fearless without hatred
Timeless and formless
Beyond birth and death
Self-existent
Known through his grace

Guru Nanak

Sikhism

PREFACE

The five hundredth anniversary of the birth of Guru Nanak in 1969 was marked by an International Seminar at the Punjabi University in Patiala. It was the first international interfaith conference that I attended. As I started to read more about Guru Nanak I was at once thrilled by the universalism of his message. Two years earlier, I had become Hon. Secretary of the World Congress of Faiths, which was founded in 1936 by Sir Francis Younghusband.

Younghusband, thanks to his travels and extensive contacts with people of different religions in the late nineteenth and early twentieth century, had become increasingly aware of the spirituality at the heart of other religions as well as in Christianity. This was confirmed for him by a mystical experience in Tibet in 1904, of which he wrote,

'I had visions of a far greater religious faith yet to be, and of a God as much greater than our English God as a Himalayan giant is greater than an English hill. But to have enjoyed the experience did not finally satisfy me. I would communicate it to all the world.'

Before I had discovered Youghusband's writings, a year's study of Indian religions at Madras Christian College in 1963, had already convinced me, as I wrote at that time, that 'all religions reflect an encounter with God who is universally present. Their response is always partial and culturally conditioned (as much in Christianity as in other faiths). All religions are continually confronted by the judgement and grace of God, particularly as His judgement and grace were expressed in the actual historical life of Jesus of Nazareth. Today His judgement and grace is experienced especially in dialogue, where people of different faiths meet each other at a deep level of their being.'

Immediately, Guru Nanak's words, after his own decisive spiritual experience, that 'I see neither a Hindu nor a Muslim, only a man' struck a chord in my heart. Guru Nanak insisted that there is One God

– even if Hindus and Muslims called God by different names. At that time, many Christians thought of Hindu and Muslim gods as different and false gods.

I was also convinced that Guru Nanak's message sprang from his own personal experience of God's greatness and goodness. At the seminar, however, there were many debates about whether Guru Nanak borrowed more from Islam or Hinduism, just as Orientalists discussed where the Prophet Muhammad pieced together his teaching. The assumption being that the message of both was put together from different sources as if they were authors writing a book, rather that interpreting an authentic encounter with the Holy One.

The International Seminar at Patiala was also marked by the opening and dedication of the Guru Gobind Singh Bhawan. The foundation of Guru Gobind Singh Bhawan was laid during the 300th birth anniversary celebrations of Guru Gobind Singh Ji. The foundation stone had been laid down by the then President of India, Hon'ble Dr Zakir Hussain in 1967. The Bhawan from its beginning has been an emblem of Punjabi University and is dedicated to promotion of peace and harmony. It is a five petalled structure in the midst of a water pool expressing different fragrances of divinity. The five identical constituent wings, designed in the style of a boat floating on water, are dedicated to the study of the major world religions. With its shared central space the layout of the building symbolizes the spirit of religious harmony. It was one of the buildings that inspired my unfulfilled dream that an International Interfaith Centre would be built in Oxford.

Because of the universalism of the Sikh message, Sikhs have played an important part in the growing interfaith movement. I have been privileged to return several times to Patiala, thanks to invitations of Dr Ahluwalia and Dr Dharam Singh and on one occasion went with some Sikhs on a pilgrimage to their holy places. It was moving experience to be with them at the Golden Temple. I took part in a seminar at the Guru Gobind Singh University in Amritsar, held to mark the four hundredth anniversary of the installation of the Sikh scriptures at the Golden Temple. I have several times been a guest at the Gobind Sadan and, at the invitation of Dr Mohinder Singh, taken part in meetings in

Delhi. I was also invited to Kirpal Sagar for the dedication of a building, which 'radiates a message of unity to the world.'

Sikhs in Britain have also made an important contribution to the World Congress of Faiths. I especially value the friendship of Pam Wylam, of Dr Chatwal, for many years editor of the Sikh Courier, of Owen Cole and of Mary Kaur. I am very grateful to Ajit Singh, MBE, and Charanjit Ajit Singh, who have given many years devoted service to the World Congress of Faiths and gave considerable time to reading a draft of this book and making valuable corrections and suggestions. Thanks too to Mary for allowing me on holiday to read a draft to her and for her valuable suggestions Mistakes and opinions are, of course, my responsibility.

It is the universalism of Sikhism that has inspired me. Largely in response to hostility and persecution, Sikhs also became a clearly defined community. Their story may help members of other faiths, as they struggle to be loyal to their heritage to recognise that there is one God, who is Father and Mother of us all and that whether, Hindu or Muslim, Sikh or Christian, Jew or Buddhist, we share a common humanity, which we are called to serve.

1. Guru Nanak

Sikhism begins with Guru Nanak. Guru Nanak was born in 1469. The probable date was April 5, but others say his birth or enlightenment was a few months later, on the full moon day of the eighth month of the Hindu calendar. In any case the festival of Gurpurab or Guru Nanak Jayanti, an important and sacred Sikh festival, is celebrated during October or November.

The late fifteenth century, in which Guru Nanak grew up, was a pause in a time of turmoil and terror in the Punjab. Earlier, the people had suffered the bloody invasions of India by Amir Timur of Samarkand - better known as Tamerlane (1336-1405). A few years later the land was invaded by Babur (1483-1530), the first Mughal Emperor. Some stability was created by Buhlul Khan, an Afghan governor of the Punjab, who seized the throne and founded the Lodhi dynasty - despite the disputes between Hindu kings. Talwandi, where Guru Nanak was born was on the direct route to Delhi. Its inhabitants, Hindus and Muslims, lived side by side. They repeatedly had to rebuild after the destruction caused by the invading armies.

Guru Nanak's father, Kalu, was a Hindu of the Kshatriyas caste (the second, warrior or merchant caste). Kalu looked after the finances of a prosperous landlord, who had converted from Hinduism to Islam. It was a happy home. His mother Tripta and sister Guru Nanaki doted on him. Stories of Guru Nanak's childhood suggest that though he played with other children, he early on showed an interest in spiritual things. When he was seven, he was taken to a pandit or teacher to learn to read – later he learned Sanskrit and also Arabic and Persian. Eventually he told the pandit that worldly learning was of little value compared to reflecting on the Name of God. Guru Nanak would often write spiritual poems in his notebook.

Guru Nanak was sometimes dreamy. Once he let the cattle, which he was supposed to be watching, wander into a farmer's field and trample down the crop. He also spent long hours in silence and his parents worried whether he was emotionally or physically ill. They were also puzzled by his questions about the meaning of traditional religious rituals.

When at eleven it was time for him as a high caste Hindu to put on the sacred thread, he enquired of the Brahmin priest what difference a thread would make. 'Was it not righteous deeds,' Guru Nanak asked, 'that distinguished one person from another?' As he did not get a satisfactory answer, Guru Nanak refused to wear the thread. He then recited to the pandit and his father's guests this verse that he had composed:

Out of the cotton of compassion
Spin the thread of contentment,
Tie the knot of continence,
And the twist of virtue;
Make such your sacred thread; (421)

As a teenager Guru Nanak was invited by Jai Ram, his sister's husband, to Sultanpur. Jai Ram found work for him as a store-keeper with his own employer, who was a high official. It is not clear whether Guru Nanak was yet married to Sulakhani, with whom he had two sons. He worked hard but was constantly aware of the Divine Presence.

God has His seat everywhere,
His treasure houses are in all places. (5)

If I remember Him, I live
If I forget Him, I die. (9)

Guru Nanak spent several years at Sultanpur. His life changed when he was nearly thirty. One morning, he failed to appear for work. Instead, after his morning ablution in the local river, he was carried away into the presence of God, who charged him to preach the Divine Name. Emerging from the river, he declared, 'There is neither Hindu nor Muslim.' In God's sight, he said, religious differences do not count. Some Muslims regarded this as an insult, but Guru Nanak successfully defended himself before a judge.

In about 1496, Guru Nanak set out on his travels. First of all he went eastward to Hardwar and Benares – both Hindus pilgrimage centres. Then he went to Assam, Orissa, Southern India and Sri Lanka. He also visited Tibet, Kabul, Mecca and Baghdad. In his discussions with scholars and mystics, he shared with them his message of the Oneness of God – as he did with people wherever he travelled.

There are many stories about his travels. At Hardwar, the Brahmins pointed out the advantages of sacrifices and burnt-offerings and of the worship of gods and goddesses, but the Guru replied that true sacrifices consisted of giving food to those who repeated the name of God and practised humility. On his travels, he would invite people to join in singing some of his hymns.

On one occasion in Sayyadpur (now Emindabad), he stayed in the house of a carpenter named Lalo. A high caste official, who had heard of Guru Nanak's fame, asked him to come to a meal. After initially declining, Guru Nanak went, but ate nothing. His host enquired, 'Why, if you eat the carpenter's food, do you not eat what I have offered you?' Guru Nanak replied, 'Your food reeks of blood, while that of Lalo tasted like milk and honey.' Asked to explain, Guru Nanak said, 'Lalo earns his food with the sweat of his brow and out of it offers whatever little he can to the wayfarer, the poor and the holy; and so it tastes sweet and wholesome. But you, being without work, squeeze blood out of the people through bribery.'(i)

In the same way, Jesus watched people putting money into the temple treasury. When he saw a widow put in two very small copper coins, Jesus said, 'I tell you this widow has put in more than all the others. All these people gave their gifts out of their wealth, but she, out of her poverty put in all she had to live on.' (Luke, 21, 2)

Guru Nanak had no use for ritual. He mocked the Hindu custom of throwing sacred water in worship toward the rising sun. He insisted that pollution was a question of behavior, not of what you touched.

Pollution of the mind is greed,
The pollution of the tongue lying,
The pollution of the eyes is to look with covetousness
Upon another's wealth,
Upon another's wife,
And the beauty of another woman,
The pollution of the ears is listening to slander. (472)

In the same way Jesus criticized the ceremonial washing practised by the Pharisees. He said to his disciples,
'Don't you see that nothing that enters a man from the outside can make him "unclean"? For it does not go into a man's heart but into his stomach and then out of his body. What comes out of a man is what makes him unclean. Out of men's hearts, come evil thoughts, sexual immorality, theft, murder, adultery… All these evils come from inside and make a man unclean.' (Matthew, 15, 12)

In Mecca, Guru Nanak lay down with his feet towards the holy Ka'aba. He was woken by a Muslim who angrily reproved him for this profanity. He said 'Turn my feet to any direction where God is not present.' He stressed inner holiness. To Muslims he said,

Make mercy your mosque
and faith your prayer mat,
Righteousness you Qur'an;
Modesty your circumcising,
Goodness your fasting,
For thus the true Muslim expresses faith.' (141)

Positively, Guru Nanak urged people to trust God and dwell on *Nam*, which is usually translated 'Name', but has a far richer meaning. *Nam* signifies the Divine presence, Reality and Truth. By living in harmony with the Divine Name, a person is freed from the circle of death and rebirth. Devotion to the Name is the way to liberation. Guru Nanak urged people to sing the praise of God. 'Oh my mind', Guru Nanak said, 'love God as a fish loves water.'

After many years of travel, Guru Nanak decided it was time to settle down and he chose Kartarpur, on the river Ravi, which is now in Pakistan. He stayed there for the rest of his life. Gradually disciples came to settle there and a community grew of people who worshipped, worked and ate together. Most of them came from the farming community of the Punjab and were usually members of the Jat caste. Some merchants of the Khatri caste and a few Muslims also joined the community. Everyone was expected to work as well as join in the morning and evening hymn singing. 'They alone who live by their own labour and share the fruit with the others have found the right path.'

The emphasis on the praise of God did not mean for Guru Nanak, unlike Hindu holy men, indifference to or withdrawal from the world. Quite the contrary; he advocated willing and joyous acceptance of life. 'The body is the palace: the temple, the house of God. Into it He has put His eternal light.' Liberation was to be won in the world, 'amid its laughter and sport, fineries and food.' He saw a divine purpose in family life and emphasised its value. 'Living in the midst of wife and children,' he said, 'one would gain liberation.' He stressed the importance of service of others. 'By a life of service in this world alone will one become entitled to a seat in the next world' 'There can be no love of God without service.'

Because the world is God's creation Guru Nanak was deeply concerned about social and economic problems of the time. He attacked the rampant corruption and abuse of power. 'The times are like a drawn knife… And righteousness hath fled on wings.(145) He criticised the rulers, yet the judges recognized that any statement by a Sikh was beyond question, as it was well known that a Sikh would never lie. He complained that religion was mostly formal and often hypocritical. 'Those who wear the sacred thread use knives to cut men's throats.' Indeed, although Guru Nanak repeatedly spoke of God's power and justice, he did once ask,

'When there was such suffering, did you not feel pity, O God?
Creator, you are the same for all.' (360)

Sikhism

Guru Nanak was disgusted by the treatment of women as inferior.

From woman man is born;
Within woman, man is conceived;
To woman he is engaged and married.
Woman becomes his friend;
Through woman, future generations come.

To woman he is bound. So why call her bad?
From her, kings are born.
From woman, woman is born;
Without woman, there would be no one at all. (473)

Guru Nanak also opposed *Sati*, a funeral custom whereby a widow immolates herself on her husband's pyre, or commits suicide shortly after her husband's death.

Before he died, Guru Nanak, rather than appointing one of his sons to be his successor, chose a devout follower called Lehna, who was a convert from worship of the Hindu goddess Durga. He renamed him Angad, meaning an 'inseparable part' of himself. With his last breath, Guru Nanak infused his spiritual light into his successor.

After Guru Nanak Dev passed away, there was a disagreement among his disciples as to who would claim the Guru's body for funeral rites. The Muslims wished to bury him while Hindus wished to cremate his body. They reached an agreement to cover his body and for Hindus to place flowers on his right side and the Muslims to place flowers to his left side. Whoever's flowers remained fresh throughout the night would perform the ceremony.

On the following morning September 22, 1539 A.D The Sikh, Hindu and Muslim devotees returned. They carefully lifted and removed the sheet which had been placed over the Guru's body. All were amazed and astonished to discover that no trace at all remained of Guru Nanak Dev Ji's mortal body. Only fresh flowers remained. Not a single bud had wilted of any blossom left by either Hindus or Muslims.

The devotees erected two separate memorials in order to commemorate Guru Nanak Dev and revere him as their own. Two shrines, one built by Sikhs and Hindus and the other by the Muslims, were placed side by side on the banks of the River Ravi in Kartarpur. Over the centuries, both shrines have been washed away by the river.

Guru Nanak is considered by Sikhs to have departed his body only. His illumined spirit is believed to be immortally divine and to have been passed on through each of the succeeding Sikh Gurus. It now forever resides, as an eternal guide to enlightenment, in the scriptures - the Guru Granth Sahib, to which as we shall see Guru Nanak made such a significant contribution.

2.   Guru Nanak's Successors

Guru Angad (1539-1552)
Guru Amar Das(1552-1574)
Guru Ram Das (1574-81)

Guru Angad

Angad, whom Guru Nanak appointed as his successor, was born in 1504 in a village called Sarai Naga, which is now in Pakistan. Like Guru Nanak, he was of the Khatri caste. It seems that he was so upset after Guru Nanak's death that he tried to go into hiding or perhaps it was to avoid the hostility of Guru Nanak's two sons, who had been passed over.

It is said that one day, Lehna, who was to become Angad, heard a neighbour singing one of Guru Nanak's hymns. His mind was captured by the tune and while on his annual pilgrimage to Jawalamukhi Temple Lehna asked his group if they would mind going to see the Guru. They refused and as he was the guide and leader of the group, he could not abandon them. Later, Lehna went one night to visit Guru Nanak. Upon receiving directions to the Guru, Lehna found a number of people working in a field. He asked one of them if he could take him to the Guru. The man agreed and took the saddle strings of the horse while Bhai Lehna sat upon the horse comfortably. After some time they reached the Guru's home and was asked sit down whilst the water was fetched. When the Guru entered Lehna realized instantly what a huge mistake he had made – the man he had been speaking too was Guru Nanak himself. Guru Nanak smiled and asked his visitor his name.

Lehna gave deep and loyal service to Guru Nanak. Several stories are told to explain why Guru Nanak appointed him as his successor rather than either of his sons. For example, when a jug fell into some mud, Guru Nanak's sons would not pick it up; one refused because the filth would pollute him, and the other refused because the task was too menial for the son of a Guru . Lehna, happily picked it out of the mud, washed it clean, and gave it to the Guru full of water.

Little is known for sure about Guru Angad. He popularized the present form of the Gurmukhi script - one of the scripts used for the Punjabi language - which he modified and standardized and used to make Guru Nanak's hymns more accessible to the people.

The institution of the *langar* or free kitchen was maintained and developed. The Guru's wife personally worked in the kitchen and served food to the members of the community and the visitors.

It is said that soon after he had lost his throne, Humayun, the second Mughal Emperor, visited Guru Angad. When he arrived Guru Angad was sitting and listening to hymns. Emperor Humayun was angry that the Guru did not get up to greet him. He got out his sword and was about to attack Guru Angad: but the Guru reminded the Emperor that when he needed to fight to keep his throne, he ran away. The Guru asked, 'Why now do you want to attack a dervish engaged in prayer?' Emperor Humayun asked for forgiveness. The Guru told him that he would eventually regain his throne but should now leave the country.

The Guru earned his own living by twisting coarse grass into rope. By so doing, he showed that even the meanest productive work is to be valued. All offerings went to the common fund. Guru Angad travelled widely and visited the Sikh communities which Guru Nanak had established. He also set up some new ones. One of his last acts was to ask a wealthy follower, Gobind, to build a new village called Goindwal, which his successor made a centre of Sikh devotion. He wrote,

To see without eyes,
Without ears, hear,
To walk without feet,
Without hands, work,
To speak without a tongue—
Thus living, yet detached from life, O Guru Nanak.
If you follow the word of your Master
You shall surely meet Him.

All the world is His dwelling place;
The True One among us resides.
Whom He wills He makes one with Himself,
Whom He wills He destroys;
By His will is one rid of illusion,
By His will another is ensnared.
And which one of us can know who shall receive his grace?
He alone finds the Supreme, whose mind he illumines. (339)

Before his death Guru Angad, following the example set by Guru
Nanak, nominated Guru Amar Das as his successor (the third Guru
Nanak) He gave him all the holy writings, including those he received
from Guru Nanak. He died on 29 March 1552, at the age of 47.

Guru Amar Das

Guru Amar Das continued Guru Angad's efforts to create a distinct Sikh
identity. Sikhs were told to gather at Goindwal for Vaisaki (Harvest
festival) and Diwali. Sikhs now had to choose between celebrating the
Hindu festival at home with families and friends or obey the Guru by
going to Goindwal. Guru Amar Das also provided an alternative to the
Hindu pilgrimage centres in Hardwar and Varanasi by digging a pool in
Goindwal. It was in a peaceful place in the forest. The pool had eighty-
four steps down to it – eighty four being the number of rebirths that a
soul experiences. Pilgrims were expected to say the Japji on every step.
He also built a mud hut for prayer and meditation.

Guru Nanak who ate with Hindus and Muslims had established the
langar or shared kitchen. Guru Amar Das continued the *langar*. This
helped to erase caste distinctions and affirm the equality of all
members of the Sikh community, but it also made Sikhs more distinct
as a community. Guru Amar Das himself ate in the *langar* as did the
Mughal Emperor Akbar when he visited Goindwal in 1567. He wrote,

Let no one be proud of his caste.
For the man who has God in his heart,
He and no other, is the true Brahmin,
So, fool, do not be vain glorious about caste,

for vainglory leads to many evils.
Though they say there are four castes,
One God created all people.
All men are moulded of the same clay.
The Great Potter has merely varied the design.(1128)

Guru Amar Das also divided the scattered Sikh communities into twenty-two districts (known as *manjis*). A leader or *massand* was appointed to look after the spiritual welfare of the Sikhs and to encourage missionary work and collecting donations. Guru Amar Das also took steps to enhance the status of women. They were prohibited from practising *sati* - the self-immolation of a widow on her husband's funeral pyre. He allowed widows to remarry and stopped women wearing veils. He also appointed some women as preachers.

All this practical action did not divert Guru Amar Das from emphasizing the spiritual message at the heart of the faith. Over nine hundred hymns in the Guru Granth Sahib are written by him, of which here are some examples:

My self, serve the Lord. Abandon service to any other.
Service of the Lord brings fulfilment of heart's desire:
Service other than the Lord's is a waste of life.
To the Lord is my love dedicated;
The Lord is my way of life! The Lord is mine!
His account my sole discourse! By the holy Guru's grace
May my heart in devotion be absorbed.
Mother, my heart is full of joy, for I have found my true Guru;
I found the true Guru following the gentle path of mystical union.
My heart resounds with cries of joy ...
I have attained bliss because The true Guru I did find.
(Anand Sahib)

Guru Amar Das was over ninety when he died in 1574. He had chosen as his successor Jetha, whom he renamed Guru Ram Das or Servant of the Lord. Jetha had impressed him by his devotion and his hard work. It is said that he served him in a spirit of complete self-surrender. He, along with his daughter Bibi Bhani, used to shampoo Guru Amar Das and draw water, cook, serve meals from the kitchen and then wash the dishes. The more he served the Guru, the more his love increased. Gradually his disposition became divine just as they say iron is turned into gold by the contact of the philosopher's stone.

Later on, when the construction of the Baoli (a well with stairs) was undertaken, Guru Ram Dass became conspicuous for his tireless and unremitting labour. He carried baskets of earth on his head like everybody else. Jetha was married to Guru Amar Das' daughter. Before he died, Guru Amar Das had told him to excavate another pool, less than a mile from the old one, which was to become the lake on which the Golden Temple is built. The pool (or tank as it is sometimes called) became the principal place of pilgrimage. Traders and artisans were invited to settle at the town so that its growth could be rapid. In time the place was to be called Amritsar.

Guru Amar Das was also a poet of great sensitivity. He composed 679 hymns in varying musical measures, which were incorporated into Adi Granth. His simple message with its emphasis on a life of selfless service rendered in a spirit of total devotion to the Guru and God, went straight to the heart.

Even in a gale and torrential rain,
I would go to meet my Guru.
Even if an ocean separates them,
A Sikh would go to meet his Guru.
As a man dies without water,
A Sikh would die without his Guru
As parched earth exults after a shower,
A Sikh rejoices on meeting his Guru. (767-8)

When Guru Ram Das died in 1581, he appointed Guru Arjan Dev to be his successor as the fifth Guru. The choice of Guru was now hereditary, but not necessarily of the first born son.

3. Guru Arjan Dev

Guru Arjan Dev's life and his martyr's death exemplify the highest virtues of Sikhism. He also gave to Sikhism its main place of worship, the Golden Temple, and its scripture which is known as the Adi Granth or Guru Granth Sahib - which are discussed in subsequent chapters.

Guru Arjan Dev, who was born near Amritsar, now in the Punjab, was the youngest son of the family. From an early age he showed a deep devotion to God, and to the envy of his brothers, he became the favourite of his father, who appointed him to be his successor. Guru Guru Arjan Dev was invested as Guru by Bhai (Revered) Budha, who was a highly esteemed devotee, on 1 September, 1581.

Guru Arjan quickly completed the excavation of the sacred pool at Amritsar, which his father Guru Ram Das (1534-81) had begun, and extended the town. He then superintended the construction of the Golden Temple, or Harimandir Sahib Sahib, which is the Punjabi for 'temple of God.' He also had a sacred pool constructed at Tarn Taran, to which many people with leprosy came to be cared for by the Guru. As he travelled, he encouraged villagers to sink wells and one of these can still be seen in the city of Lahore.

Under Guru Arjan's leadership, Amritsar became a place of pilgrimage, a centre of learning and the focus for all Sikhs. This was strengthened by the Guru's decision to collect the hymns of other Gurus in what is known as the Adi Granth and place them in the Golden Temple. Guru Arjan spent much of his time preaching in the Punjab and deepening his devotion to God. As he wrote in one hymn,

Meditate, meditate, meditate,
Thereby peace is obtained and Worry and anguish are expelled,
Remembering God, you're not reborn.
Remembering God, the fear of death is dispelled.
Remembering God, death is eliminated.
Remembering God, your enemies are repelled.

Sikhism

Remembering God, no obstacles are met.
Remembering God, night and day, you're fully awake.
Remembering God, fear cannot touch you.
Remembering God, you don't suffer sorrow.
Remembrance of God, with the Saints,
All treasures are Blessings from the Lord. (262)

Soon after the completion of the *Adi Granth*, Guru Arjan was summoned to the presence of the Mughal Emperor, Akbar (1542-1605) - a man of wide religious sympathies. Complaints had been made that the book was derogatory to Islam. The book was opened at random. A passage from a place pointed out by the Emperor was read. The hymn was in praise of God, as were the subsequent passages. Akbar was delighted and gave the Guru generous gifts. The Guru's importance was also recognised by Fr. Jerome Xavier, who in a letter to the Governor of Goa said the Guru's status was similar to the Pope's

Akbar's successor, the Emperor Jahangir, was by no means so broad-minded. His enthronement took place one week after his father's death on November 3rd, 1605 - (two days before the Gun Powder Plot in England). In the struggle for the succession, Jahangir had promised the Muslim scholars (*Ulema*) to protect the Muslim religion. He also was uneasy about the growing independence of the Sikh community. The Emperor seems to have been influenced by Sheik Ahmed, the head of the revivalist Naqshbandi Sufis, who had no sympathy for 'those who believed Ram and Rahman (the Merciful One) were the same.' Whereas Guru Arjan in one of his hymns had said,

Some remember God as Ram;
Some call him Khuda; (a Persian word for Lord)
Some use the name Gosain,(a Hindi word for Lord).
Some worship him as Allah.
Gracious Lord, Almighty,
You are the source and cause of everything,
O Lord, Compassionate One,
Shower your grace on all...
Whoever does the will of God,
To him all things are revealed.' (885)

Chandu Shah, a senior adviser to Lahore's Mugal Viceroy, also voiced the Brahmin opposition to the Sikhs for undermining caste distinctions.

Emperor Jahangir regarded the Guru as heretical and disloyal. It is not clear, however, whether Jehangir acted for religious or political motives. In the Emperor's diary, Tuzuk-i-Jahangiri, he noted that on being told his rival for the throne, Khusrau, had been received by the Guru and that there had been some correspondence between them, Jehangir notes, 'We became convinced that the man was a charlatan and a false prophet.' Jehangir ordered that Guru Arjan be arrested, his property confiscated and that he be 'dealt with in accordance with the penal Laws of *Yasa*.'

One of the laws of *Yasa* was that a priest and a person of exalted spiritual status should not be put to death in any way that caused the shedding of their blood and that such a severe penalty was only to be used if the safety of the state was in danger.' 'This was a clever move of Jehangir,' according to Professor Prithipal Sing, 'because it indicated that Shariah law had not yet been made the sole medium of Mughal governance under him. '(ii)

This confirms the view of Professor P. S. Kapur Singh that the conflict was primarily a 'Mughal-Sikh conflict,' although it came to be seen as a Muslim-Sikh one. Mughal Emperors, he points out, from the time of Babar avoided religious persecution. Babar in his advice to his son had exhorted him to avoid religious fanaticism and do justice to people of every creed according to their beliefs. 'Do not destroy temples or kill animals. This is the only way to control the people of India.' Incidentally, the East India Company forbade missionaries from entering its territories for fear they would cause disturbance. (iii)

Whatever his motivation, Emperor Jehangir had Guru Arjan brought to Lahore. There he was tortured by being made to sit on red-hot iron plates and by having burning sand poured over him. He was then taken to bathe in the river Ravi, but the shock of cold water on his blistered body, was too much for him. Even as he walked to his death, he recited the words, 'Your will is sweet, Oh God; I only seek the gift of Your Name.' A Jesuit priest in Lahore wrote at the time, 'their good Pope died, overwhelmed by sufferings, torments and dishonours.' He was the first Sikh martyr. One of his contemporaries wrote,

As fishes are at one with the waves of the river,
So was the Guru, immersed in the River that is the Lord.

The death, of Guru Arjan, marked a turning point in Sikh history. Growing persecution by Muslim rulers led Sikhs to take up arms in self-defence and eventually to the creation of the Khalsa. The teaching of Guru Nanak was preserved in the scriptures but at a popular level inspiring stories about their lives, *janam-sakhis*, began to circulate. Even if historically inaccurate, they popularized the Guru's message.

3. The Later Gurus

Guru Hargobind, 1606-1644,
Guru Har Rai, 1644-1661,
Guru Guru Har Krishan, 1661-1664,
Guru Teg(h) Bahadur, 1664-1675

Guru Harbogind

With the martyrdom of Guru Arjan and growing hostility from the Mughal Emperors, significant changes took place in the life of the Sikh community. The event, it has been said, turned a peaceful movement of reconciliation into the most militant ever witnessed in India.

Guru Arjan's parting message to his son Guru Hargobind, who was only eleven years old when he succeeded his father, was 'Not to mourn or indulge in unmanly lamentations, but to sing God's praises,' but he also advised him 'to sit fully armed on his throne and to maintain an army to the best of his ability.' Out of this emerged Guru Hargobind 's concept of giving equal time to spiritual (*meeri*) matters and secular (*peeri*) concerns. Guru Hargobind quickly set about obtaining the best horses and weapons and started training camps for swordsmanship, archery and physical education.

Not all were happy with these developments. Bhai Gurdas, Guru Arjan's faithful disciple, voiced this unease: 'The earlier Gurus sat peacefully in sacred places (*dharamsalas*); this one roams the land. Emperors visited their homes with reverence; this one they cast into jail. No rest for his followers, ever active; their restless Master has fear of none. The earlier Gurus sat graciously blessing; this one goes hunting with dogs. They had servants who harboured no malice; this one encourages scoundrels.'

At once, however, Bhai Gurdas affirms his loyalty:
'None of these changes conceals the truth; the Sikhs are still drawn as bees to the lotus. The truth stands firm, eternal, changeless, and pride still lies subdued.' (iv)

Besides his spiritual responsibilities, Guru Hargobind also created the Akal Takht ('The Almighty's throne') to be a meeting place for representatives to organise the *panth's* (community's) secular and military affairs. Its meeting place, also called the Akal Takht, was in Guru Hargobind's time only an earthen embankment. It had a raised platform on which the Guru sat to receive those who wanted to consult him on important matters. The area also became an open-air forum for debate. Years later, the Akal Takht was to become a five storey building with a gold-leafed dome, over-looking a marble paved square.d marble.

Emperor Jahangir was alarmed by these developments and sent troops to arrest the Guru, whom he detained at Gwalior Fort. Before his own release, the Guru had also obtained the release of the many Hindu feudal chiefs who had been detained there for a few months.

When Guru Hargobind was released he did not change his policy. Soon armed conflict took place and initially the Sikhs were successful. Guru Hargobind, however, realising that the new Emperor Shah Jahan sought his life, decided to leave Amritsar so as to avoid any risk of the Golden Temple being damaged. He never returned to the Golden Temple.

Guru Hargobind now travelled widely – engaging in skirmishes with the Mughal army, but also visiting many Sikh communities, encouraging them to strengthen their faith by building places for prayer and worship. He built two towns – Hargobindpur and Kiratpur. He died in 1644 and was succeed by Guru Har Rai, who had been born in 1630. Guru Har Rai was a saintly man and travelled widely to spread the teaching of Guru Nanak. He did not himself write any hymns.

Guru Har Rai

When Aurangzeb, a zealous Muslim, became Emperor, he sent for Guru Har Rai, who had offended Aurangzeb by receiving his elder brother Dara Shikoh - a rival for the throne. Hai Rar refused to go, saying, 'I am not a king who pays you tribute, nor do I want anything from you, nor are we like a disciple. Why have you summoned me?'

Instead he sent his son Ram Rai, who when he was reciting a passage from the scriptures slightly changed some words which were critical of Islam. Guru Har Rai was so annoyed that his son had dared to change the words of the *Adi Granth* that he refused to see him again.

Guru Har Kishan

Guru Har Rai, therefore appointed his younger son Guru Har Krishan to be the eighth Guru, even though Guru Har Krishan was only five years old. Sadly, the young Guru died of small-pox three years later in 1664 – soon after Charles II had been restored to the throne in Britain.

Guru Tegh Gahadur

The youngest of Guru Hargobind's sons, Tegh Bahadur, now became Guru. It is said that before he died Guru Har Krishnan uttered the word *'Baba Bakala.'* This was thought to be a message that the next Guru was living in the village of Bakala. Indeed, after Guru Hargobind's death, his wife had taken her son to her parents' home in Bakala.

Guru Teg Bahadur had a mystical nature but was also a good horseman and showed his bravery at the battle of Kartarpur. He travelled widely, to Bengal, Assam and Dacca (now in Bangladesh), which he called 'a citadel of Sikhism,' and to many other places. In his travels, besides encouraging Sikhs, he also spent time visiting the centres of India's other faiths. For example, he visited Bodh Gaya, where the Buddha gained enlightenment.

In 1672, after his travels, Guru Teg Bahadur created a new settlement at Chakk Guru Nanaki, named after his mother. The place later came to be known as Anandpur, which became, as I realised when I visited it, a formidable stronghold.

By this time Aurangzeb's hatred for all who were not Muslim was increasing. In 1669, according to his chronicler Mustaq Khan, issued this proclamation, 'His Majesty, eager to establish Islam, issued orders to the governors of all the provinces to demolish the schools and temples of the infidels and with the utmost urgency to put down the teachings and public practice of these misbelievers.' This meant putting down or killing the leading 'infidels.'

Iftikhar Khan, the governor of Kashmir, rigorously enforced this decree. He used force to convert some of the Hindu teachers (*pandits*) to Islam. Other teachers went to Amarnath to ask for the help of the Hindu god Shiva. In a dream, one of them was told by Shiva to go to the Punjab and ask for help from Guru Tegh Bahadur. When they appealed to the Guru for help, he pondered the matter deeply. Indeed his son, who was only nine, asked his father why he was so preoccupied. He replied: 'Grave are the burdens the earth bears. She will be redeemed only if a truly worthy person comes forward to lay down his head. Distress will be expunged and happiness ushered in.' Gobind Rai replied, 'No one could be worthier than you to make such a sacrifice.'

After listening with sympathy to the pandits, Tegh Bahadur declared that if Aurangzeb persuaded him to convert, then the pandits would do the same. Aurangzeb in response, ordered that Tegh Bahadur should be 'fettered and detained' and brought to Delhi. Tegh Bahadur set out of his own will to Delhi, but was arrested on the way. His captors tried by argument and torture to get the Guru to convert.

The Guru's challenge to the Emperor was simple. 'The Prophet of Mecca who founded your religion could not impose one religion on the world, so how can you? It is not God's will.'

On November 11 1675, The Guru was forced to watch his three close companions being cruelly killed: one was sawn alive, the second was boiled to death and the third was burnt alive. On the same day Tegh Bahadur was publicly beheaded – on the place where, years later, the Gurdwara Sis Ganj Sahib in Delhi's Chadni Chowk was built.

Appropriately, Guru Teg Bahadur had written these words which are included in the Guru Granth Sahib :

The truly enlightened ones
Are those who neither incite fear in others,
Nor fear anyone themselves. (1427)

On the night of the Guru's execution there was a wild storm which allowed some of his followers to recover his head which they then took to Anandpur and gave to his nine year old son. The Guru's head was then ceremoniously cremated on a sandalwood pyre to the chanting of verses from the Adi Granth. The Guru's body, during that same stormy night, was taken by Lakhi Shah Lubana: as it was too dangerous to have a formal cremation, he put the body in his house and then set fire to his own house. The Gurdwara Rakab Ganj Sahib, near Parliament House in New Delhi, which was built in 1783 by the Sikh military leader Baghel Singh (1730–1802), marks the site of the cremation.

4. Guru Gobind Singh

Guru Tegh Bahadur, before he died, symbolically appointed as his successor Gobind Rai, (better known as Guru Gobind Singh), who was only nine. He was formally installed on 29 March 1676.

Recognising the amazing generosity of Guru Tegh Bahadur in risking death to help members of another religion, Guru Gobind Singh was to write:
He gave his head for men of faith without flinching
and chose martyrdom in the cause of righteousness.

His father's death shaped his son's future actions and convinced him that the tyrant's injustice and cruelty had to be resisted by courageous warriors.
When all other means have failed,
It is but lawful to take to the sword. (iv)

Guru Nanak had said 'truth is pure steel.' Steel is a symbol of determination and strength of character. St Paul also urged Christ's followers to 'Put on the full armour of God ... and take the sword of the Spirit, which is he word of God.' (Ephesians 6,18). Guru Gobind Singh said the same, putting his trust in the steel of the sword and writing;
You are the subduer of kingdoms,
The destroyer of evil armies...
I seek your protection ...
I cherish you, the saviour of creation,
Hail to you, O Sword. (490)

Writing in the middle of the nineteenth century, J.D. Cunningham, rightly observed that Guru Gobind Singh 'resolved upon awakening his followers to a new life and upon giving precision and aim to the broad and general institutions of Guru Nanak. In the heart of a powerful empire he set himself the task of subverting it, and from the midst of social degradation and religious corruption he called up simplicity of manners, singleness of purpose, and enthusiasm.'(v)

As an adolescent Guru Gobind Singh, who was trained in swordsmanship, enjoyed martial games. He also learned several languages and had a gift for writing. In due course he wrote his autobiography. He used his poems to teach love, morality and loyalty.

While he gave the Sikhs a distinct identity, he also recognised the unity of the human race, as he wrote in his poem *Akal Ustat:*

Recognise all mankind as one,
Whether Hindus or Muslims,
The same Lord is the creator and nourisher of all:
Monastery and mosque are the same,
So is Hindu worship and Muslim prayer.
Men are all one.

Guru Gobind Singh's teenage years were ones of preparation. In 1685 he went to stay with the friendly Raja of Sirmur State for three years. As a young man, he was described as 'sharp featured, tall, superbly dressed, with a plume-topped turban and always armed.'

The next twelve years were ones of conflict. The Sikhs were caught up in the rivalry of local rajas. In 1690, the Mughal rulers moved against those rajas, who had stopped paying their dues to the court. By this time, however, Guru Gobind Singh had reinforced his base at Anandpur and built a hill fort to strengthen its defence. He joined with those rajas who were opposing the Mughal's army. The Sikhs played a vital part in the Mughal's defeat.

Then in 1693, the Emperor Aurangzeb, who was increasingly angered by Guru Gobind Singh's activities, ordered his military commanders to prevent the Guru from assembling his followers. Defiantly, Guru Gobind Singh ordered Sikhs, even from distant communities, to gather at Anandapur for the New Year (Baisakhi) celebrations. The Sikhs were to come bearing arms and with uncut beards – to distinguish them from Muslims, who cut their beards. Yet, although the Mughal army attacked the rajas, they left the Sikhs alone. From 1697 to 1700 there was some respite from fighting. This gave Guru Gobind Singh time to take measures that would give the Sikhs greater strength and unity.

On 30 March 1699, Guru Gobind Singh convened another great gathering of Sikhs at Anandpur. Here is the traditional account, although some scholars question it. (vi) The Guru appeared in front of a crowd of some 80,000 with a naked sword and asked, 'Is there present a true Sikh who would offer his head to the Guru as a sacrifice?' There was an awed silence. He repeated the question twice. On the third occasion, Daya Ram arose and walked behind the Guru to a tent nearby. Soon the Guru reappeared with his sword dripping blood. He asked for another head. This was repeated until five men had offered their lives to the Guru.

Soon afterwards they were led back from the tent dressed in saffron coloured raiment with neatly tied turbans and with swords at their side there. The Guru said to them, 'My brothers, you are in my form and I in yours. He who thinks that there is any difference between us errs exceedingly.'

The Guru then dissolved sugar crystals in water, which he stirred with a double-edged sword, reciting the *Japji* and other sacred songs at the same time. He then initiated the 'The Five Beloved Ones' (*Panj Pyare*) with *amrit*, the nectar of immortality, asking them to repeat after him

Waheji ka Khalsa, Waheji ki fateh. (The Khalsa are the chosen of God, Victory be to our God.)

Guru Gobind Singh himself received initiation from 'the five beloved ones' All five were called Singh and became the first members of The Khalsa - the name of the body of initiated or pure Sikhs. They were required to wear five symbols of the *Khalsa,* all of which began with the letter 'k': *kes*, long hair and beard; *kangha*, a comb to keep it tidy; *kara*, a steel bracelet; *kachch*, short breeches and *kirpan*, a sword. Their appearance distinguished them from both Muslims and Hindus and gave the Sikhs a visible and separate identity. During the next few days, some 50,000 Sikhs were initiated.

It is sometimes said that as the Guru was stirring *amrit*, two sparrows dipped their beaks in it. They then flew off and killed a hawk. There is a saying, 'Through entering the Khalsa, sparrows become hawks.'

The *Khalsa* of Singhs ('lions') and *Kaurs*, (the name for women which probably means 'princess') was to be a casteless and disciplined community, resisting the its enemies and supporting the oppressed and those in need. People of every caste and creed were to be treated equally; they were to be faithful in marriage and not to cut their hair or smoke. (vii)   At the formation of the Khalsa, Guru Gobind Singh outlined the way of life of the Khalsa, in what is sometimes called the *Rahit*. This consisted of a summary of Sikh teachings, rules of personal behaviour, details of Khalsa ceremonies and sanctions for those who offended against the rules. Guru Gobind Singh also voiced his hopes for the Khalsa and gave Sikhism an identity quite distinct from Hinduism.

Three reasons are often given for the founding of the Khalsa. It is said that after Guru Tegh Bahadur's execution, some Sikhs disguised themselves in case they were killed as well. Guru Gobind Singh, therefore, was determined to make sure that Sikhs would be instantly recognizable and could not hide when danger threatened.

The second reason, according to the eighteenth century Rata Singh Bhangu, was that, because the Sikhs were seen as peace-loving and an easy prey for their enemies, Guru Gobind Singh, instead, wanted his followers, known by the name of Singh (or lion), to appear as 'splendid warriors.' He introduced a rite of initiation (often called baptism) which was administered with a sword. This was to create a Khalsa that was staunch and unyielding. 'His followers would destroy the empire, each Sikh horseman seeing himself as a king.' (viii)

The third reason was the need for administrative reform, partly because of the growing number of Sikhs and their wider dispersion. The original *manji* religious administrative units had often allowed deputies (*masands*) to act for them - many of whom were corrupt. Instead, the Guru wanted to centralize power and place the whole community directly under his control. He made clear that he had no confidence in the *massands*, saying 'If anyone serves them, they tell him "Fetch and give us all your offerings"...Those beasts plunder men, and never sing the praises of God.' (*Dasam Granth, Swayyas* 29 and 30)

These developments, however, alarmed the neighbouring princes. They asked Aurangzeb to expel the Sikhs from Anandapur. 'Should you delay, his next expedition will be against the capital of your empire.' The Mughal army, with support from the princes, quickly started a prolonged siege of Anandapur.

When the water supply was cut off, the situation became desperate. At this point Aurangzeb offered safe conduct if the Sikhs agreed to leave Anandapur. In an autographed letter the Emperor wrote, 'I have taken an oath on the Qur'an not to harm you. If I do, may I not find a place in God's court hereafter! Cease warfare and come to me. If you do not desire to come hither, then go whithersoever you please.' The Emperor's envoy added that the Emperor promised not to harm the Guru. The hill Rajas also, calling their gods to witness, swore that they would allow safe passage to the Guru. The Guru told the enemy, 'You are all liars, and therefore all your empire and your glory shall depart. You all took oaths before and then perjured yourselves.'

Some Sikhs went to the Guru's mother to complain of his refusal to listen to reason, but he urged them to be patient, 'O dear Khalsa, you are rushing to your destruction, while I am endeavouring to save you.' Some Sikhs, however, were beginning to waver in their allegiance to Guru Gobind Singh. Only forty Sikhs decided to remain with him and share his fortunes. He told them that they too might desert him, but they refused and said that they would either remain within the fort or force their way out as he directed. Guru Gobind Singh now knew that the seed of his religion would flourish, so he then finally decided to leave Anandpur and gave his men orders to march at night.

The moment the enemy got the news of the Guru's departure, they, as before, forgot all about their pledges and immediately set out in hot pursuit. Many Sikhs were killed as they tried to escape. Many more lost their lives at the battle of Chamkaur. The Guru himself escaped after the battle and after a terrifying night alone, he met up with three of his companions. They finally reached safety when a local Muslim chief welcomed them: but they then heard the tragic news of the horrific death of his mother and two young sons, who had refused to convert.

Guru Gobind Singh wrote two forceful letters in Persian to Aurangzeb, denouncing his deceitful behavior: 'I do not approve of what does not accord with ethical principles and the dictates of conscience.' Aurangzeb, who was in the Deccan, invited him to meet him: but before Guru Gobind Singh had travelled far, the ninety-one year old Emperor died. He did meet his successor, Bahadur Shah, in Agra in 1707 and had a cordial time with him. Gobind Singh then went to Nander.
Guru Gobind Singh, nonetheless, still had powerful Muslim enemies. One evening in October of the following year, as the Guru rested after the prayer-time, two Pathan assassins attacked and wounded him. Before his death, he told his followers to revere the scriptures as their Guru. The *Adi Granth* now became known as the *Guru Granth Sahib*. He assured them that 'Wherever there are five Sikhs assembled who abide by the Guru 's teaching, know that I am in the midst of them: the Guru is *the Khalsa* and the *Khalsa* is the Guru.' The decisions of the Khalsa were, of course, subject to the scripture.

Yet, although the future of Sikhism lay with the Khalsa, it seems that at least well into the nineteenth century there were Sikhs who kept to the ways of the earlier Gurus. Indeed, it is paradoxical that a movement, which began with Guru Nanak who said that religious differences had no meaning in God's eyes, should itself have become a distinct religious community. Guru Gobind Singh's actions also pose the unanswerable question of whether Truth is best served by martyrdom – and his mother and sons were martyred - or by the sword. Yet without Guru Gobind Singh's courage and leadership, the Sikh community and faith might have been destroyed, whereas it is becoming increasingly influential as Sikhism, with many adherents in all parts of the world. Dr Sarvepalli Radhakrishnan (1888-1975) a philosopher and a President of India, said that the creation of the *Khalsa* planted the seeds of India's independence: 'India is at long last free... This freedom is the crown and climax and a logical corollary to the Sikh Gurus' and *Khalsa's* terrific sacrifices and heroic exploits.'

5. The Golden Temple

My first sight of the Golden Temple in 1969 was tantalizingly brief. After the International Seminar in Patiala to mark the anniversary of the birth of Guru Nanak, we set out for a visit to Amritsar. On the way, however, we stopped to see the beautiful Gurdwara at Tarn Taran, a school and other places, so that it was evening before we reached Amritsar. Some of us were booked on the night train back to Delhi.

Happily I have been back on other occasions and each time I have been overwhelmed by its beauty. On one World Congress of Faiths tour, we were greatly honoured by being shown the beautiful and precious gifts that have been given, over the centuries, to the shrine. They are housed in the treasury (*Toshakhana*). On another occasion some members of the World Congress of Faiths went with Sikh friends on a pilgrimage to the Temple. We spent the night in a simple Pilgrims' lodge so we could get up early to share in the daily devotions.

I was also there at a seminar, at the Guru Nanak University in Amritsar, which was to coincide with the four hundredth anniversary of the installation of the Granth Sahib in the Harimandir. The crowds were so enormous - in the region of three million people - that we watched the ceremony on television. The President, the Prime Minister, and religious leaders of all faiths were there. The next morning, however, we visited the shrine when it was a little less crowded.

The Harimandir, rather like the Vatican, is a complex in which each building has its own name. The excavation of the Sacred Pool (*Amrit Sarovar*) was begun by Guru Ram Das in 1573. A few years later he founded a small settlement, which in time became the city of Amritsar. He bought the land from local landlords (*Zamindars*). There is a tradition that the site was an ancient holy place with rejuvenating waters. There is a story that a person with leprosy was cured by bathing in it. The place may have been visited by Guru Nanak. All this is uncertain. What is certain is that the foundation of the actual temple, usually called the *Harimandir Sahib (or Harmandir Sahib)*, took place in 1589 – *Hari* is a name for God.

According to an early Sikh tradition the foundation stone of the Harimandir Sahib was laid by Guru Arjan himself. A later and now commonly accepted tradition is that Guru Arjan asked a Muslim Sufi saint Hazrat Mian Mir of Lahore to lay the stone. The construction work was directly supervised by Guru Arjan Dev, who was assisted by prominent Sikh personalities as well as many devotees.

A solid foundation was laid, to raise the building up from the bottom of the pool. Broad walls were built and a bridge connected the temple to the side. The main structure of the Harimandir Sahib, functionally as well as technically, is a three storied one. The front faces the bridge and is decorated with repeated cusped arches. The first floor is at the height of just over 26 feet. At the top of the first floor a 4 foot high parapet rises on all the sides which has also four small domes (Mamtees) on the four corners and exactly on the top of the central hall of the main sanctuary rises the third story. It is a small square room and has three gates. A regular recitation of Guru Granth Sahib is also held there. Above this room stands the low fluted dome, with a lotus petal motif in relief at the base and an inverted lotus at the top.

The building was completed in 1601. To celebrate the occasion, Guru Guru Arjan Dev sang this song:
O saints, beautiful is the tank of Guru Ram Das;
Yea, whosoever bathes in it,
his whole progeny is blest...
Bathing, his mind is at peace,
For he contemplates God, his Lord. (623)

A large number of Sikhs participated in the work of building the Golden Temple. They were rewarded with *Bakshishes* (honorariums). Some of the devoted Sikhs became shining examples of the faith.

Instead of building the Harimandir Sahib on a higher level as was the custom of traditional Hindu temple architecture, he built it on a lower level than its surrounding ground so that the visitors would have to go down the steps in order to pay homage to the holy shrine and to show humility in God's presence. Another distinguishing feature of the structure of the Harimandir Sahib was that unlike the Hindu temples which usually have only one gate, the Harimandir Sahib was made open on all the four sides to show that entry was open to all - of every caste and faith.

The object of Guru Arjan in planning the structure of the Harimandir Sahib in the middle of the Amrit Sarowar was to combine both spiritual and temporal aspects to represent a combination of the Nirgun (unknowable) and Sargun (revealed) concepts of God.

While the construction work was going on, the news about the outstanding project of the unique pilgrimage centre under construction spread far and wide. Sikhs, in large numbers, began to visit Amritsar, which soon attained the status of a great holy place,. The praise of the newly constructed holy place spread far and wide. Local Sikhs visited the temple daily; Sikhs of the nearby areas did so frequently and those of distant places twice a year on the occasions of Diwali and Baisakhi.

The next remarkable development of the Harimandir Sahib was the installation of the scripture of the Sikhs – the *Adi Granth* - described in the next chapter. Unlike Hindu temples, there is no statue of a god. Instead, there is a holy book.

The Adi Granth, which came to be known later as the Guru Granth Sahib, was formally installed in the Harimandir Sahib in August 1604. Baba Budha was appointed the first Granthi (headpriest) of the temple. Regular worship, Kirtan and other services of the shrine started at once. Soon the Harimandir Sahib became the principal place of worship, unparalleled in beauty and glory. As Guru Arjan sang:
I have seen all places;
there in not another like thee,
For thou wert established by the Creator-Lord,
who Blest thee with Glory...
Thou art of unparalleled beauty,
And whosoever batheth in thy tank, is rid of his sins (1363).

In the eighteenth century the Temple was three times attacked and desecrated by Muslim rulers (1757, 1762 and 1764). Each time it was cleansed and restored. Its present design dates from its restoration in 1764 by Jassa Singh, who was born in 1718. At the age of thirteen, he inherited the wealth of Ahluwalia *Misl* - one of the sovereign states of the Sikh Confederacy. In 1747, he was given the command of the Khalsa army and even his enemies admired his courage. In time he established himself as the recognised leader of the Sikh community and Sikhs regarded it as a privilege to be initiated by him. Jassa Singh was as devout as he was courageous. He often visited to worship at the Harimandir Sahib and largely, at his own expense, he restored the temple after its repeated desecration by Afghan invaders.

A few years later the *Darshani Doehri,* which is the gateway to the path that leads across the water to Hamandir Sahib, was built. On the upper floor is the *Darshani Doehri* or treasury. Soon a circumambulatory pathway (*Parkarma)* was constructed and also a canal was made to bring water to the temple.

The Harimandir Sahib got the name of Swaran Mandir (Golden Temple) when its upper part was sheathed in richly embossed and highly gilded sheets, for which Maharaja Ranjit Singh paid. The architecture of the Golden Temple represents the highest achievement of the Sikhs in art and architecture. The allied arts of decoration and frescoes inside the temple display the skilled craftsmanship of the Indian artists of the nineteenth century.

The Golden Temple is not only a place of worship but a rallying centre for the whole Sikh community. It embodies the heritage of the Sikh people gathered over five hundred years history. Legends and miracles are connected with the holy tank while great martyrdoms and triumphs are associated with various places in the temple precincts. The temple was a symbol of the Sikh struggle for independence in the eighteenth century. In the nineteenth and twentieth centuries all important Sikh movements have originated in the precincts of the Golden Temple.

In the early nineteenth century Maharajah Ranjit Singh took much interest in the temple and, as already mentioned, gave money for the gilding and decoration of the Harimandir Sahib. Several Europeans visited the temple during these years, including the Austrian Baron von Hügel, a Roman Catholic layman and modernist theologian. He noted that 'places of pilgrimage are so numerous in India that they are only noticed by the government for the sake of levying a tax on pilgrims' but the Sikhs were so poor 'that they had nothing from which tax could be levied.' Even so, Hügel admired the way that the Sikhs had restored the temple and cared for it.

The British were respectful of the shrine, but kept a watchful eye on the Temple management committee. As one colonial official said, 'From the annexation of the Punjab the great political importance of the Darbar Sahib has been acknowledged by the Local and Supreme Governments and it has been considered of paramount importance that the Government should retain some active control over the appointment and operations of the Committee of Management.' (x) The British, therefore, were keen to see that the manager was pro-British, as was the case with the Sirdar Jodh Singh, the first manager that the British appointed and who served from 1849-1862. The British also wanted to avoid offending Sikh sensibilities and reacted strongly against three drunken British employees who disgraced themselves by smoking, spitting and urinating in the holy place. The Governor-General said that 'such conduct on the part of English men brings disgrace on our nation.'

By the end of the nineteenth century, Sikh reform movements were gaining strength and increasingly they wanted to take full control of the Golden Temple. Eventually in 1921 control of the Harimandir Sahib was given to the Shiromani Gurdwara Prabandhak Committee (SGPC). The Sikh Gurdwara Act was passed four years later in 1925.

Sadly, in the twentieth century, the Golden Temple has, on three occasions, been a witness to violence. The Jallianwala Bagh massacre in 1919, which took the life of many innocent Sikhs, happened not far from the holy building. Then after the partition of India in 1947,

Amritsar became a border town and many Sikh refugees came to the city. The most shocking event was the invasion of Golden Temple under operation 'Blue ˉStar.' In 1982, Jarnail Singh Bhindranwale, who campaigned for a semi-independent Sikh state, with some 200 armed followers, moved into a guest-house in the precinct of Harimandir Sahib. By 1983, the Harimandir Sahib became a fort for a large number of militants. *Time* magazine described Amritsar in November 1983 as closely resembling 'a city of death. Inside the temple compound, violent Sikh fanatics wield submachine guns, resisting arrest by government security forces. Outside, the security men keep a nervous vigil, all too aware that the bodies of murdered comrades often turn up in the warren of near-by streets.'

According to the Indian government, Operation Blue Star was launched to eliminate Jarnail Singh Bhindranwale and his followers who had sought cover in the Amritsar Harmandir Sahib Complex. The Indian Army stormed Harimandir Sahib Sahib on the night of 5 June under the command of Kuldip Singh Brar. The forces had full control of it by the morning of 7 June. There were many casualties, both of soldiers and civilians and militants, including Bhindranwale himself.

It is said that Britain provided highly detailed advice to the Indian authorities on a helicopter-borne SAS-style operation to seize the Golden Temple. The advice was ignored by the Indian army, which launched a ground assault, which caused a heavy loss of life.

In 1988 there was further trouble, but the twentieth century also saw improvements to the Golden Temple. On three occasions there have been complete cleansings of the holy water (*Ka Sewa*).

In 1949 a Sikh Reference library was formed and nine years later a Central Sikh museum. Then In 1998 a large number of near-by shops were removed to make a corridor around the Golden Temple. This new space has added to the beauty of the Golden Temple, which has subsequently been completely restored and re-gilded.

A year before Queen Elizabeth II and Prince Phillip paid a visit to the Golden Temple, after they had laid a wreath at Jallianwala Bagh. Gurcharan Singh Tohra, president of Sikhism's ruling body, said: 'The Queen's visit will send the message around the world that peace prevails in the Golden Temple.'

Inevitably one describes the Golden Temple in terms of history and architecture, but Satish K Kapoor in his *Golden Temple* is right to say that the 'Harimandir Sahib is not hallowed simply because of its antiquity or splendour ... but because the Holy Word resounds in it day and night. Its sanctity lies in the fact that it has led men and women towards divinity and noble virtues like service and sacrifice. An aura of Infinite spiritual force gives devotees a sense of the Supreme.' It has rightly been called 'a spiritual marvel in architecture.'

6. The Guru Granth Sahib

As a religious community, establishes its own identity, it has to distinguish between its authentic message and that of others who misrepresent or pervert that teaching. The early Church recognised four gospels as authentic. Other so-called gospels were regarded as apocryphal – or inauthentic even if they were supposed to be by St Peter or another disciple. In the same way al-Bukhari sifted through many *hadith* or stories about the Prophet Muhammad, and out of some two hundred thousand selected only about three thousand.

The best known name for the Sikh scriptures is the Guru Granth Sahib. Granth means a holy book, from Sanskrit *grantha* 'literary composition', which is derived from *granth* 'to tie' or so to bind a book. Sahib is a term of respect, such as 'Sir' or 'Master.' The title indicates that the book is the guiding principle of Sikh faith and practice, taking the place of human Gurus.

The hymns now to be found in the Guru Granth Sahib were written by several of the Gurus. Guru Nanak sent his to the scattered Sikh communities for use in morning and evening prayers. His successor, Guru Angad, began collecting his predecessor's writings.

This tradition was continued by the third Guru, Amar Das. Besides the hymns of the three Gurus the collection - often referred to as the Goindwal *pothis* (books) - some hymns of Muslim and Hindu devotional poets, such as Kabir, who disregarded distinctions of caste or creed, were also included. (Goindwal was where Guru Angad lived).

When Guru Arjan discovered that pretenders - including his elder brother who was resentful that he had not been chosen as - started circulating their own hymns as if they were those of previous Gurus, he decided to make a collection of their authentic hymn.

The book of the hymns of the first three Gurus was in the possession of Guru Amar Das' elder son, Baba Mohan, whose grandson had copied the hymns. Baba Mohan, it seems, had not approved of his father's choice of Guru Ram Das to be the next Guru.

He was, therefore reluctant to allow Guru Arjan, a son of Guru Ram Das, to have access to the collection of hymns. So, Guru Arjan, went to ask for them from Baba Mohan, who was of a mystical nature and who had shut himself in the upper room of his house in Goindwal.

Guru Arjan, to the accompaniment of a stringed instrument, chanted a hymn outside Baba Mohan's window. Mohan was so moved by this that he agreed to lend the collection to Guru Arjan, who later returned it to the family.

Guru Arjan already had copies of his father's hymns. He then sent messengers to some of the places that Guru Nanak had visited to bring back any previously unknown writings. He also invited members of other religions and contemporary religious writers to submit writings for possible inclusion. The next task was to select the hymns to be included.

Rejected submissions were ones in which the author blasphemously identified himself with God, were derogatory to women, or advocated withdrawal from the world.

Bhai Gurdas, Guru Arjan's scribe, knew the criteria. When Guru Arjan asked him to submit his own compositions, he replied that he was not worthy of such an honour. The Guru admired his honesty and said 'Your works shall be the expositional key to the Pothi Sahib.(xiii)

To this considerable collection of the hymns of previous Gurus, Guru Arjan added over two thousand of his own compositions. The best known of these is his *Sukhmani* (Hymn of Peace), which is read daily in worship and also to the dying to comfort them. It emphasises the spiritual peace that comes from constant recollection of God's name.

The Hymn of Peace consists of twenty-four poems of eight stanzas. The first stanza of the first poem ends with this refrain:

The Name of God is sweet sustenance,
Source of Peace and Joy within;
The Name of God brings perfect peace
To those who are truly devout. (262)

Guru Arjan also provided this epilogue:
Three things are there in the vessel;
truth, contentment and intellect.
The ambrosial Name of God is added to it,
The name that is everybody's sustenance.
He who absorbs and enjoys it shall be saved.
One must not abandon this gift,
It should ever remain dear to one's heart.
The dark ocean of the world
Can be crossed by clinging to His feet.
Guru Nanak, it is He who is everywhere. (1428)

In 1604 the manuscript of this collection, usually known as the Adi Granth, was complete. The time had come for it to be installed in the Golden Temple. This took place on 16 August 1604. The book was carried to the Golden Temple in a reverent procession. Guru Arjan walked beside it, waving a fly-whisk over it. When the procession reached the Temple, the sacred book was placed on a platform. The Guru sat, humbly, beside it on the floor. The elderly Bhai Buddha, a great scholar, who had known Guru Nanak, recited some of the hymns. Guru Arjan insisted that, unlike the Hindu scriptures, the Pothi Sahib could be open to reading by anyone of any caste, creed or sex.

Still today, the *Guru Granth Sahib* is placed on a platform in the Golden Temple. Throughout the day musicians sing the hymns and a fly-whisk is waved over the holy book. Three hours before midnight, the book is closed, wrapped in clean sheets, and taken ceremoniously to the Akal Takht to rest. At dawn, after the Temple has been washed, the holy book is brought back and the singing resumes. (In many Hindu temples also the gods are given time to rest).

It is customary for devotees to prostrate themselves in front of the scripture. It was a moving experience when I went with some Sikh friends on a pilgrimage to the Golden Temple to be present at the ceremonies. Prostrating myself before the Guru Granth Sahib made me more aware of the reverence due to all sacred scriptures.

Owen Cole said of the compilation of the Adi Granth and its installation in the newly built Golden Temple by Guru Arjan that it had two consequences.

'First, it reiterated the distinction between the human and the message in a visual way which must have made an impact on his followers, especially if, as tradition asserts, he bowed before the volume as he installed it and instructed his followers to imitate his example.' The Guru himself is reported as saying "The Granth is a ship across the ocean of the world, those devoting their hearts to it shall swim across. As the Guru's person in all places shall not be visible, know the Granth to be the Guru's heart. Its significance is deeper than that of my own self; know it to be your lord and show it reverence."

Secondly, the compilation of the Adi Granth began a process whereby Sikhs were to become a people of the book to an extent and in a manner which is not found in any other religion.' (xiv)

The celebration to mark the four hundredth anniversary of this event, which I had the privilege of attending, attracted over a million people including both the President and Prime Minister of India, as well as dignitaries of many religions.

It is an interesting coincidence that 1604 is also a significant date in the history of the Bible – at least for those who speak English. In that year, King James I ordered a new translation to be made of the Bible into English, which became known as the Authorised Version or King James Bible. In the Dedication to King James and in the Introduction, the importance of translating the Bible into the language of the people (rather than insisting on Latin, which only scholars understood) is strongly argued. In the same way, Guru Arjan rejected the use of Sanskrit – the language of the Vedas.

Although the sixth, seventh, and eighth Gurus wrote no religious verses, Guru Tegh Bahadur, did. The tenth Guru, Guru Gobind Singh, although he did not include any of his own verses, wanted to add Tegh Bahadur's songs to the holy book. This was not without difficulty. The original Pothi Sahib (known today as the Kartarpur Bir) had been kept by Guru Hargobind in his house. From there it was stolen by his grandson Dhir Mal, who wanted to use it to further his claims to be the rightful Guru. Thirty years later the followers of Gur Tegh Bahadur forcibly recovered it, but were told by the to return it. They placed it in the shallow river bed of the Satluj River, where Dhir Mal recovered it unharmed: but, later, Dhir Mal refused to let Guru Gobind Singh see it, saying 'If you are a Guru, then prepare your own.'

So, during a lull in the fighting with Emperor, Guru Gobind Singh retired to Talwandi Sabo, and proceeded to dictate by memory all the verses to Bhai Mani Singh. He then added the hymns of his father, Tegh Bahadur. This version is known as Damdami Bir.

Guru Gobind Singh's own hymns were collected by Bhai Mani Singh and placed in a separate book, the *Dasam Granth*. This contains biographical material, four compositions that express the militant piety of Guru Gobind Singh, a panengyric, an 'Inventory of Weapons' and some legendary material. The Dasam Granth is regarded as scripture, but it does not have the authority of the Guru Granth Sahib. Some of Guru Gobind Singh's religious verses are included in the daily prayers of Sikhs. Here is one example:

He is in the temple as He is in the mosque,
He is in Hindu worship as He is in Muslim prayer... Hindus and the
Muslims — are all one.
People have different homes,
But all men have the same eyes,
The same body, the same form compounded of the same elements—
Earth, air, fire and water.

Thus the Brahman of the Hindus
and the Allah of Muslims are one,

The Quran and the Vedas praise the same Lord.
They are all of one form, the one Lord made them all.

The great task of re-writing the entire Guru Granth Sahib was finally completed in 1705. It was then taken to be installed at Nanded, which is located on the banks of the River Godavari in Maharashtra.

It was there that Guru Gobind Singh died. The inner room of the gurdwara, which was built between 1832 and 1837 by order of Maharaja Ranjit Singh (1780– 1839), called the *Angitha Sahib*, is over the place where Guru Gobind Singh was cremated in 1708.

Before he died, as we have seen, Guru Gobind Singh, realising that he would die of the wounds inflicted by two assassins, instead of appointing a successor, said that in future the scriptures would be their Guru. Just as some previous Gurus had taken five coins and a coconut to place before their successor, Guru Gobind Singh did the same before the scriptures, which soon became known as the Guru Granth Sahib. Bhai Nand Lal one of Guru Gobind Singh's disciples recorded these words of Guru Gobind Singh:

He who would wish to see the Guru,
Let him come and see the Granth.
He who would wish to speak to him,
Let him read and reflect upon what the Granth says.
He who would wish to hear his word,
He should with all his heart read the Granth.'

After Guru Gobind Singh died, Baba Deep Singh and Bhai Mani Singh prepared many copies of the new Damdami Bir. The main collections of manuscripts of the Guru Granth Sahib are listed by Dr Mohinder Singh in the beautiful book, *Guru Guru Arjan Dev*: *Life, Martyrdom and Legacy.*

What happened to the original manuscript is still debated. In 1849, the British, who had annexed the Punjab, discovered a copy with its golden stand in Lahore. 'Out of respect and deference to the British Government,' a copy was made and presented to Queen Victoria. It is now in the India Office Library.

The first printed copy of the Guru Granth Sahib was made in 1864. Great care is taken while making printed copies. Any copies of Guru Granth Sahib with misprints are cremated. Since the early 20th century, the Guru Granth Sahib has been printed in a standard edition of 1430 *angs* (pages). Translations may have different paginations, but they usually also show the traditional number of the page.

A partial English translation of *Guru Granth Sahib* by Ernest Trump was published in 1877. The work was for use by Christian missionaries, but received extremely negative feedback from Sikhs. This was partly because he smoked cigars in the presence of Sikhs, who regarded tobacco as taboo: also because Trump, who did not consult with religious leaders, 'paid little attention to the traditional renderings of the hymns of our Gurus and saints' as the Khalsa Divan said in their welcome address to Lord Curzon.

Max Arthur Macauliffe also partially translated the text for inclusion in his six-volume *The Sikh Religion*, which was published by The Oxford University Press in 1909. Despite some inaccuracies, his translations are closer to the Sikhs' own interpretation and were received well by them. Maccauliffe, indeed, said that one of his main objectives in writing his *The Sikh Religion* 'was to make some reparation to the Sikhs for insults which he (Trump) offered to the Gurus and their religion.'(xvi)

The first complete English translation of the *Guru Granth Sahib,* by Gopal Singh, whom I had the honour of meeting, was published in 1960. He presented a copy to the Pope. A revised version published in 1978 removed obsolete English words like "thee" and "thou". There have been a number of subsequent translations. The *Khalsa Consensus Translation* is popular and is used on major Sikhism-related websites.

The entire Guru Granth Sahib is written in the Gurmukhi ('from the mouth of the Guru') script, which, as have seen, was standardized by Guru Angad Dev in the 16th century. The Gurmukhī script is one of the official scripts in the State of Punjab.

Apart from the opening invocation or *Japji*, the hymns are arranged by *Ragas*, which are a combination of notes associated with different moods and times.

There are thirty one ragas in the *Guru Granth Sahib* – Macauliffe gives the melodies in Western notation. Under each raga, the hymns are arranged in accordance with the historical order of the Gurus. There are also some devotional hymns by Kabir and other Hindu bhakti poets and by some Muslim Sufis.

Sikhs consider the *Guru Granth Sahib* to be a spiritual guide not only for Sikhs but for all of humanity; it plays a central role in guiding the Sikh's way of life. Its place in Sikh devotional life is based on two fundamental principles: that the text is the living Guru and that all answers regarding religion and morality can be discovered within it. Its hymns and teachings are called *Gurbani* (sometimes *ki bani*) or "Word of the Guru".

7. 1708-1799

The 250 years from the birth of the first Guru to the death of the tenth Guru laid the lasting foundations of Sikhism, rather as the time of the Apostles and Church Fathers moulded the history of Christianity. Yet however much a faith community claims authority from the past, its continuing life is shaped by the ever-changing context in which it is practised.

The century that followed the death of Guru Gobind Singh was a time of great challenge for Sikhs and the survival of the Khalsa. Before his death Guru Gobind Singh told the Sikh communities to rally around Banda Singh's banner, although some groups, such as the ascetic Udasi sect kept apart.

Banda was probably born in Kashmir in about 1670. He was a farmer and then abandoning the world, he adopted the ascetic way of life of a Hindu sadhu and settled in the city of Nander in western central India, in what is now Maharashtra state. Guru Gobind Singh met him there and converted him about a month before he died. When Banda set out for the long journey to the Punjab he had only twenty five followers. But he also had Guru Gobind Singh's directive and the five arrows that he had given him.

As he journeyed north, Sikhs from various places rallied to him. After a few successful skirmishes, Banda headed for Samana, a town of hateful memories for Sikhs. It was the home town of Sayyed Jalal-ud-Din, who had ordered the execution of Tegh Bahadur. Although the town was heavily defended, Banda's surprise attack was successful. So many people were killed that 'pools of blood flowed through the drains.' Further victories added to the confidence that Sikhs now had in him and in themselves.

Banda then turned his troops against the Sikh's old enemy Wazir Khan. Banda approached Sirhind, the principal town of South-East Punjab. It was there that Guru Gobind Singh's two younger sons had been bricked up alive. After a ferocious battle, Banda captured Sirhind, but spared the lives of most of its Hindu population.

As Banda's power increased and he gained control of most of the Punjab, the Emperor grew anxious. In 1712 the Emperor Bahadur Shah died.

After the usual struggle for succession, Muhammad Farrukh Siyar became the new Emperor. At once, he sent orders to his commander Zakariya Khan 'to expel Banda from Sadhaura or if possible to destroy him altogether.' Despite heavy losses, Zakariya Khan recaptured Sadhaura and Lohgarh, and sent his son to Delhi to present the Emperor with the heads of many Sikhs who had been killed. Banda, himself had avoided capture. After further battles, the outnumbered Sikhs retreated to Gurdas Nangal, where they hastily built fortifications and held out against their enemies for eight months.

Their courage even gained the admiration of their enemies. The chronicler Muhammad Qasim wrote that 'the brave and daring deeds of the infernal Sikhs were wonderful. Twice or thrice a day...when the imperial forces went to oppose them, they made an end of the Mughals with arrows, muskets and small swords.' When the end came, it was due more to starvation and illness.

The Sikhs, finally, surrendered in December 1715. 300 Sikhs (or in account 2,000) were immediately executed and their heads then 'stuffed and mounted on spears'. These, with Banda manacled in an iron cage on the back of an elephant, were taken in procession to Lahore then to Delhi, where, by the time they arrived there were 748 prisoners in heavy chains. There the executions began early in March.

It was not until June 9th that Banda himself was killed. First, they put his child in his arms and told him to kill it. He refused, so they 'ripped open the child before his eyes, thrust its quivering flesh in his mouth. They then hacked Banda to pieces' (xvii). The Gurdwara Shahidi Asthaan Baba Banda Singh Bahadur near Delhi's Qutab Minar marks the place.

Although Banda is mostly remembered for his military exploits, he also abolished the *Zamindari* system, by which landlords with extensive holdings, often exploited the peasants who had no proprietary rights over they land they cultivated. Banda, instead, gave them, most of whom were *Jats*, ownership of their land.

The Sikhs now suffered a period of oppression and persecution from the Muslims. When Zakariya Khan became governor of Lahore, he offered a reward of fifty rupees – in those days a very large sum - for every Sikh head brought to him: but, loyal to Guru Granth Sahib and the Khalsa, Sikhs held firmly to their faith.

Seeing that persecution did not work, in 1733 Zakariya Khan offered the Sikhs their own principality (*jagir*). Kapur Singh, a guerrilla leader, aware of how much blood had been shed, accepted the offer. He organized the various Sikh militias into what is called the Dal Khalsa. There were two groups - one was for veterans who were over forty and the other was for younger men. They were ordered to protect places of worship, conduct initiation ceremonies and offer armed resistance.

All too soon, Zakariya Khan changed his mind. He seized Amritsar, plundered the Golden Temple and set fire to it; he then filled the pool with dead animals; and killed the head priest, Bhai Mani Singh, who was a scholarly companion of Guru Gobind Singh.

The invasion of India in 1739 by Nader Shah of Persia (1736–47), the founder of the Afsharid dynasty of Persia, who sacked Delhi, relieved the pressure on the Sikhs, who renewed their attacks. Even so, Zakariya Khan handed over the Golden Temple to the local landlord Massa Ranghar. One evening when partying with his friends, he was murdered by a Sikh. An attempt to assassinate Zakariya Khan was unsuccessful.

The persecution of the Sikhs intensified under Shah Nawaz Khan and his successor, Mir Mannu. Thousands of Sikhs were massacred in 1747 at the first disaster (*Ghalughara*), which Sikhs equate with the Holocaust.

The situation grew even worse for the Sikhs after the first of the eight invasions of India by Afghanistan's ruler, Afghan Ahmed Shah Abdali. The Mughals accepted his annexation of Lahore and Kashmir: but the Sikhs, refused to acknowledge him.

When in 1757 Abdali again invaded India, the Sikhs plundered his baggage train and rescued hundreds of captured Hindu women. Abdali reacted angrily by desecrating the Golden Temple – demolishing the Harmandir Sahib, defiling the sacred pool and killing many Sikhs. He appointed his son Timur Shah to be governor of Lahore and told him to exterminate the 'accursed infidels.'

The Sikhs took their revenge. Baba Deep Singh, who had been baptized by Guru Gobind Singh and was by then 75 years old, felt that it was up to him to atone for the sin of having let the Afghans desecrate the shrine. He emerged from scholastic retirement and declared that his intention was to rebuild the temple. Five hundred men came forward to go with him. Baba Deep Singh offered prayers before starting for Amritsar: 'May my head fall at the Temple.' His wish came true. Baba Deep Singh, although mortally wounded, reached the Golden Temple. He died on the path around the holy pool. The place on the pavement surrounding the pool is marked and Sikhs from around the world pay their respects there. Baba Deep Singh's double-edged sword, which he used in his final battle, is still preserved at Akal Takht.

In 1761, when Abdali had returned to Afghanistan, the Sikhs for a time recaptured Lahore; but on his return Abdali took his revenge and thousands of Sikhs were killed in the Great Disaster (*Wada Ghalughara*). He then attacked Amritsar, again destroying the Golden Temple and filling the pool with the dead. Next year, Charat Singh, whose grandson Ranjit Singh would establish the Sikh Empire recaptured and purified the shrine. All too soon, Abdali returned and again desecrated the shrine. The Sikhs still refused to surrender. In 1765 they recaptured Lahore and declared their sovereignty over the Punjab.

Amritsar was declared to be their mint city and institutions of government were established. Twelve *misls*, semi-autonomous states, formed the Sikh confederacy. Agriculture, manufacturing and trade were developed. The Punjab became quite prosperous. An officer of the East India Company said the area was 'exceedingly well cultivated.'

There were problems with neighbouring princes, some rivalry between the *misls* and further Afghan aggression. There was also increasing contact with the British, who eventually ended Sikh independence but not before the heyday of Ranjit Singh's Sikh Empire.

9. Ranjit Singh

Ranjit Singh, who was blind in one eye, once said, 'God intended that I look upon all religions with one eye; that is why I was deprived of the other eye.' He was careful not to alienate his many Muslim subjects. He continued to give state aid to the leading mosques and confirmed the jurisdiction of Islam law over the Muslims. He appointed both Hindu and Muslim officers in the army and both his home and his foreign ministers were Muslims.

His was a splendid court. Ranjit Singh put as much energy into enjoyment as he did into battles. His feasting was notorious. He had some twenty wives - partly to secure alliances.

Besides maintaining control of the Sikh chiefdoms, Ranjit Singh had to deal with Western imperial powers; mainly with the British, whose influence and ambition was steadily growing and to a lesser extent with the French and Russians. His own chiefdom lay on the direct route of invading armies from Afghanistan and beyond. Increasingly also, the Marathas in the south-east and the Kangra chiefs in the north and the Gurkhas in the north east were also a threat as well as the Afghans in the north-west.

This is not the place to deal in detail with the many battles, political alliances and intrigues of his reign. They are dealt with in great detail in *The History of the Sikhs* by Joseph Davey Cunningham, a courageous British author, who was an officer in the army of the East India Company and also had special responsibilities for relations with the Sikh kingdom. He wrote his book because he wanted 'to give Sikhism its place in the general history of humanity.' For his exposure of the deceitful tactics of the British, he was, removed from political office and returned to his regiment in disgrace. He died within two years, at the age of 39, of a broken heart. (xviii)

The issue between the British and Ranjit Singh was what should be the boundary of their respective spheres of influence. The river Sutlej, on which Ludhiana lies, seemed a natural boundary, but Ranjit Singh was tempted to move towards the river Jumna and the British wanted to cross the Sutlej. British officers were divided between those who wished to reach an agreement with the Sikhs and those who favoured an expansionist programme.

Despite a successful expedition south of the Sutlej, in 1809 Ranjit Singh agreed to withdraw and the two sides affirmed their 'perpetual friendship.' Ranjit Singh has been criticised for the weakness in agreeing to this treaty, but, as Patwant Singh says, 'his moves were based on clear- headed perception of his adversary's potential: on his knowledge of British artillery, ammunition, equipment... and the drill and discipline of the Company's troops.(xix) His was a wise decision. Charles Metcalfe (later Baron Metcalfe) who negotiated the agreement said to Ranjit Singh, 'Your Excellency will reap the fruits of the alliance with the British in a period of twenty years.'

Unthreatened from the South, Ranjit Singh was free to pursue conquests in other areas. In less than twenty years, the vastly expanded Sikh kingdom came to include Kangra, Attock, Multan, Kashmir, Dejarat and Peshawar. Before his death, his flag would fly in Ladakh and on the fort of Kabul.

Towards the end of his life, Ranjit Singh once again drew back from hostilities with Britain over influence in Sind. By the 1830s, his health was deteriorating. In 1825, he was very ill with malaria, but made a good recovery. Ten years later, he had a severe stroke and another in 1837. The third stroke came on Christmas Eve 1838, when George Auckland (First Earl of Auckland), who favoured a policy of agreement with the Sikhs, was visiting Lahore. His health continued to get worse so in June 1839, he made clear that his eldest son Kharak Singh should succeed him and be assisted by his chief minister Raja Dhyan Singh.

Even in his last hours, one English writer noted, that 'so deep and sincere were the feelings of respect and attachment with which he was universally regarded that to the last the most implicit obedience was paid to his commands and (when he could no longer speak) to the signs by which his will was expressed.'(xx)

Ranjit Singh became unconscious on 26 June 1839 and died the next day, but not before gifts of great wealth were given to shrines and places of worship. He was cremated the next day. Four of his wives burned themselves on his funeral pyre – although such a practice had been strongly denounced by the Gurus.

Was empire achieved by sacrificing the teaching of the Gurus? The scholar Kapur Singh has said that Ranjit's Singh first mistake was 'to assume the un-Sikh title of Maharaja.' One might also ask, 'Was subsequent British expansion and aggrandizement also achieved by sacrificing morality?'

10 Surrender to the British

All too soon internal Sikh disputes made their empire an easy prey for an even more powerful empire. Ranjit Singh's Sikh Empire did not long survive his death. Within ten years, the Punjab was under British control - partly due to internal rivalries in the Sikh community and partly to deceptive and sometimes dishonourable behaviour of the British. (*See map of the Sikh Empire 1839-49 at end of book on p. 128.*)

Kharak Singh's dissolute way of life made him totally unfitted for leadership and was 'a disastrous successor to an illustrious father.'(xxi) It has been said of him that he had 'nothing to attract or attack.' Immediately after his death, six months after Ranjit Singh had died, his half-brother Sher Singh gained British support for his claims to succeed and Kharak Singh's son Nau Nihal Singh, who was 'intolerant of the British,' also asserted his rights. Infighting amongst the Sikh leaders weakened the community.

The British, on the grounds that the situation endangered operations in Afghanistan and 'their need for the passage of troops' through Sikh territory, began to interfere. Although the Sikh Empire was an ally, already secret estimates were being made of 'the force required for the complete subjugation of the Punjab.' British ambitions were helped by what Sikhs regard as the treachery of Lal Singh and Teja Singh, high-ranking officers who worked with the British and, in Kapur Singh's words, 'paved the way for the eventual Sikh en-slavement ' (xxii).

In December 1845, the British Governor-General, Lord Hardinge, declared war on the Lahore Court (Darbar). The fighting at Ferozeshahr on December 21 was ferocious. By the evening the British army was 'near to a defeat which could have involved annihilation' – to quote the British General Sir Hope Grant. On the following day, however, Teja Singh refused to attack the dispirited British and, in the words, of General Sir Henry Havelock, 'India was saved by a miracle.' Even so, over a fifth of the British force had been killed or wounded. Prime Minister Sir Robert Peel spoke sadly of the heavy losses sustained in the fight with 'the most warlike men in India.'

By the Treaties of Lahore in 1846, the British gained the Sikh territories south of the river Sutlej and made the continuing Sikh Kingdom into a virtual British protectorate. The treaty was short lived and by the end of 1848, the new Governor General, The Earl of Dalhousie, declared a war that was generally regarded in London as illegal.

The Second Anglo-Sikh War began with heavy British defeats at Ramnagar and Chillianwala. (Wellington, aged 88, offered to go to India to take command). Despite hesitations in London, Dalhousie was determined to secure 'the entire subversion of the Sikh dynasty and the absolute subjection of the whole people.' All British resources were called upon for the Battle of Gujarat: 56,000 infantry, 11,000 cavalry, plus heavy guns against a Sikh force of 20,000 men. Sikh losses were very heavy. They retreated to Rawalpindi, where they finally surrendered to the British in March 1849. Some British 'observers who watched the surrender were impressed by the bearing of the Sikh soldiers, who still carried themselves with pride. They were tired and hungry but their spirit was not broken.'

Dalhousie now argued strongly for the annexation of the whole area and got his way. On March 30 all Sikh lands were placed under British sovereignty. The Maharajah Dalip Singh was given a pension. His property was confiscated to pay the East India Company what the war had cost them. When the British annexed the Punjab, the Maharajah was made to give the famous Koh-i-noor Diamond to Queen Victoria as a symbol of his submission to her. Dalhousie told London, 'I do not recollect any subject has fallen on the good fortune of sending so precious and so storied a trophy of war as the Koh-i-noor.' I wonder if the Maharajah felt he had been so fortunate.

After the diamond was handed to Queen Victoria, it was exhibited at the Crystal Palace. But the 'Mountain of Light' was not as shiny as the other cut gemstones of that era and there was a general disappointment regarding it. In 1852 the Queen decided to reshape the diamond and it was taken to a Dutch jeweller.

Sikhism

Following the Indian Mutiny of 1857, which the Sikhs did not support, the government of India was transferred from the East India Company to the Crown. The position of Governor General was upgraded to Viceroy, and, under the Royal Titles Act passed by Disraeli's government in 1877, Victoria became Empress of India. Queen Victoria wore the diamond occasionally afterwards. She left in her will that the Koh-i-noor should only be worn by a female queen. Later it was set in the crown of the Queen Mother. There have been many demands by Indian governments for the return of the diamond. In 2016 India's solicitor, to everyone's surprise, told the Supreme Court that India should forgo its claims because the jewel was given to Britain as a gift by an Indian king in 1851, rather than stolen.

To return to Dalip Singh: by the 1880s he was feeling isolated and complained that his income was inadequate. Then in 1886 he announced his intention to visit India, but the British made clear that he would not be allowed to visit the Punjab. He, therefore, made a public statement to the Sikhs asking for their forgiveness and acknowledged his submission to 'Sat, who governs all destiny and is more powerful than I his erring creature.' Dalip Singh had converted to Christianity when he came to England, but on a visit to Aden was 're-baptised' as a Sikh. In 1887, he visited the Czar in Russia, but had a cool reception. On returning to England he was pardoned by Queen Victoria and his pension was restored. He died in 1893.

11. British Rule

Once in control, the British set about dismantling the army, although they were soon glad to recruit Sikhs into the British army. By June 1849, they also established a governmental structure under three commissioners. The country was divided into seven Commissionerships and 27 Districts. The District Officer was responsible for collecting revenue, keeping the peace, dispensing justice and developing the District. Such development did much to improve agricultural production and the construction of metalled roads, post and telegraph systems and, soon, also railways.

Of particular importance was the innovative development of canal colonies to provide constant irrigation of much of the Punjab. The first canal, which irrigated the densely populated cities of Amritsar and Lahore, was opened in 1861. This programme has been of permanent value to the Punjab, which by early in the twentieth century was producing a third of British India's wheat, as well as a large quantity of cotton. Still today, the Punjab is one of the most fertile and prosperous areas of the country. Land in the canal colonies was given to ex-soldiers and servicemen and this encouraged large numbers of Sikhs to join the army. Legislation also prohibited the transfer of agricultural land to non-agricultural use.

The British were keen to avoid antagonizing the Sikh community. The Punjab was a frontier state and the British were afraid of incursions from the North by Afghanistan and even Russia. This concern, as we have seen, was reflected in their policy towards the Golden Temple.

The growing prosperity of the area benefitted both the local population and even more so their British masters. British missionaries were soon active and made a valuable contribution to improving educational and medical facilities. One outstanding example is The (Women's) Christian Medical College and Hospital in Ludhiana, which I have visited. It set a new standard of excellence in the area.

The number of converts was small: about 4,000 in 1881 and 300,000 in 1921. A recent census suggests that just over one percent of the population of the Punjab is Christian, although some evangelical churches say that their members have been excluded from this figure. I recall on one visit to Amritsar eventually finding the Church of North India church, which had a very small congregation, mostly of Christians from South India. Christian missionary activity also had the unintentional effect of encouraging members of India's other religions to take a new interest in their own religion. This was true of Sikhism.

One reform group, the Nirankari movement grew out of the teaching of Baba Dyal Singh (1783-1855), who preached against the assimilation of other religious traditions into Sikhism – especially the worship of Hindu gods. He emphasized the Formless (*Nirankar*), quality of God. When Dyal Singh, at the ageof 18, experienced enlightenment, he heard a voice saying: 'Give up this ritualistic practice. You have been commissioned to expel the darkness of ignorance. You are a true Nirankari.' Baba Dyal's movement was originally confined to the Rawalpindi area. His followers were not expected to live a life of renunciation. The Nirankari were typically traders and shopkeepers and were expected to continue working while they focused their attention on the remembrance of the Divine Name.

Baba Dyal's successor, Baba Darbar Singh, collected and recorded the Baba Dyal's essential teachings and established Nirankari communities outside of Rawalpindi. When Sahib Rattaji (1870-1909) was leader, they were estimated to number in the thousands and there are still some followers today.

The Sant Nirankaris belong to a separate spiritual movement which seeks to unite humankind. In the words of Sat Baba Hardev (1954-2016) 'true religion unites, never divides.'

The Namdharis, another reform movement, was started by Bhai Balak Singh (1785-1862). Little is known about him, but his spirituality attracted followers of whom Baba Ram Singh (1811-1885), who had served in Ranjit Sing's army and had fought against the British, became the leader. His study of Sikh history and letters made him well aware of the neglect of the Gurus' teaching that was at the time corroding Sikh society. He set about purging corruption and reforming society.

Ram Singh organised his followers into districts and this and his antipathy to all things British, alarmed the new rulers, who kept a close watch on his activities. Widespread arrests and imprisonments of his followers, who opposed the slaughter of cows and attacked butchers' shops in Amritsar, created a dangerous situation. The perpetrators were hanged, although one of them was thought by the Kukas to be innocent. Further violent incidents took place and then in January 1872, about a hundred Kukas attacked the government treasury and killed seven policemen and an officer. In revenge more than sixty Kukas – without trial – were lined up by the Deputy Commissioner of Ludhiana - soon dismissed from service - and blown apart by canon fire. Ram Singh was deported to Rangoon, where he died in 1885. The Kukas continue as a sect within Sikhism, observing the way of life taught by Ram Singh.

Namdharis believe that Guru Gobind Singh went into seclusion after surviving the attempt on his life and passed the Guruship to Balak Singh and his successors. Namdaris are strict vegetarians and adopt a simple way of life. They rise early, bathe and then meditate, often using a woolen rosary of 108 beads. In their worship, in which music plays a large part and which is sometimes ecstatic they repeat God's name. The men are distinguished by their white, "round" turbans with their ears fully exposed. Namdahris have a beautiful and peaceful centre at Bhaini Sahi, which I have had the privilege of visiting. There are centres in Britain and some other countries.

These two initiatives, which emphasised spiritual renewal, attracted a number of followers, but it was the Singh Sabha movement that became the main-stream response to the British influence. There were however, continuing difficulties in defining who was a Sikh. In some areas of the Punjab in 1855, Sikhs had been classified as Hindus. Again in 1898, the Punjab High Court, in a judgement on a contested will, ruled that Sikhs should be regarded as Hindus.

One point at issue was whether Sikhs who had not been initiated into the Khalsa counted as Sikhs. The answer was a tentative yes: they were called Sahaj-dharis, which means 'slow-adopters' and implied that they were on their way to full membership of the Khalsa. Subsequently the definition was narrowed to exclude Sahaj-Dharis.

British officers needed a much simpler test. For them a Sikh should have uncut hair and abstain from smoking, although the 1911 census allowed a person to register as a 'Sikh-Hindu.' In 1918 the Montagu-Chelmsford Report, which introduced representative bodies, allowed anyone who claimed to be so to register as a Sikh. By 1925, however, under pressure from the Akali campaign, a person who claimed to be a Sikh had to make this declaration, 'I solemnly affirm that I am a Sikh, that I believe in the Guru Granth Sahib, that I believe in the Ten Gurus, and that I have no other religion.' To this, the Delhi Gurdwara Act of 1971 added the requirement to 'keep un-cut hair.'

After the 1925 Act, the British lost interest in the issue, but the Shiromani Gurdwara Parbandhak Committee (SGPC) continued the task. Eventually, in 1950 the SGPC published a document, called *Sikh Rahit Maryada*, which defined a Sikh in this way:
'A Sikh is any person who believes in the Akal Purakh; in the ten Gurus (Guru Nanak to Guru Gobind Singh); in the Shri Guru Granth Sahib, other writings of the ten Gurus, and their teachings; in the Khalsa initiation ceremony instituted by the tenth Guru; and who does not believe in any other religious doctrine.' (xxiv)

Significantly, belief in the Khalsa initiation ceremony was now included in the definition, although there was some question whether a person has actually had to have taken part in such a ceremony. This meant that a Kes-dari and perhaps a Sahaj-dhari Sikh might be included.

To return, however, to the late nineteenth century, the Singh Sabha movement helped affirm Sikhs identity and confidence in their religion. It actively opposed Christian missionary work, Western education and 'representative politics.' The Singh Sabha made clear the primacy of rational thought and behaviour that fitted the Gurus' teachings.

The first Singh Sabha was founded in Amritsar in 1873 by scholars and land owners – known as Sanatanis. They regarded anyone as a Sikh who followed the Gurus' teachings, even if they did not observe the five Ks. The Lahore Sabha, established in 1879, was stricter. It opposed the worship of Living Gurus or of the descendants of the Ten Gurus and insisted upon observance of the five Ks, thereby making clear the distinctiveness of the Sikh community. By the end of the century there were over one hundred Singh Sabhas.

Other initiatives had the same purposes. The Tat Khalsa, which dated back to the eighteenth century, regained its importance, rejecting with great determination any Hinduizing practices which had been adopted by some Sikhs. Sikh faith, the Tat Khalsa insisted, had to rest on the Granth and Gurdwara. To this end the Khalsa College was established in 1897 and a number of schools. The Khalsa also, rivalling the methods of Christian missionaries, set up printing presses and published books, magazines and newspapers. The Singh Sabha and Khalsa Diwan together set up the Chief Khalsa Diwan, which provided scholarly leadership to the Sikh community.

By 1920, however, leadership had passed to Shiromani Gurdwara Parbandhak Committee (SGPC), which was more radical and impatient. In partnership with the Shiromoni Akali Dal, which was founded in 1920 and became a political rather than a religious movement, determined efforts were made to regain control of the gurdwaras many of which had been taken over by hereditary care-takes or *mahants* – some of whom were Hindu. The caretakers were backed by the British.

The Sikhs were also infuriated by the fact that the Golden Temple was controlled by a British Deputy Commissioner. His appointed manager allowed idols to be placed in the temple and Hindu pandits to teach there. Moreover lower caste people were now prohibited from entering.

An increasing number of Sikhs joined protest marches. Although they were peaceful, the British authorities became alarmed and arrests were made. In 1922, before a large congregation, the keys to the

Golden Temple were handed to the President of the SGPC. It was another three years before the Gurdwara Act gave control of their holy places to the Sikhs. The struggle was successful, but 40,000 Sikhs spent time in prison and 400 were killed. Ghandi described the struggle as 'the first decisive battle for India's freedom.'

There were other clashes with the British. The most known is the shameful Jallianwala Bagh massacre, which caused lasting damage to Sikh-British relations. Estimates of the number of those killed vary from about four hundred to over one thousand.

The Imperial Government was introducing repressive laws which led Gandhi to launch a non-violent disobedience campaign against them. In Amritsar there was a general strike. About twenty protestors were killed by police fire. Some of the crowd retaliated by attacking government properties and five Europeans were killed. The army was called in and arrived, under the command of Brigadier-General Dyer on April 11th. On the 12th Dyer issued an order banning all public meetings.

The next day was the Baisaki festival. A large crowd gathered in the Golden Temple to celebrate the birthday of the Khalsa and then moved to Jallianwala Bagh, which was completely enclosed by high buildings, to hear some speeches. Dyer entered with his army and taking position on a raised terrace next to the only entrance/exit, without warning, ordered the troops to fire onto the densely packed crowd. In the subsequent enquiry, Dyer said it only took him thirty seconds to decide what to do. He ordered the troops to fire - even on those trying to escape.

The tragedy was scarcely reported by the British press. Eventually the Hunter Enquiry criticised Dyer and the House of Commons demanded his dismissal. The right wing *Morning Post*, however, had a collection for him, which raised over £26,000. Memory of the atrocity has lived on. The massacre made a mockery of British Justice and was the moment when Jawaharal Nehru realized 'how brutal and immoral imperialism was.'(xxv). It also drew more Sikhs into the struggle for freedom.

On 13 March 1940, at Caxton Hall in London, Udham Singh, an Indian independence activist from Sunam, who had witnessed the events in Amritsar and was himself wounded, shot and killed Michael O'Dwyer, who had been the British Lieutenant-Governor of Punjab at the time of the massacre and who had approved Dyer's action and was believed to be the main planner. Dyer himself had died in 1927.

Although there has been no official British apology, Queen Elizabeth II spoke about the events at a state banquet in India on 13 October 1997, saying, 'It is no secret that there have been some difficult episodes in our past – Jallianwala Bagh, which I shall visit tomorrow, is a distressing example. But history cannot be rewritten, however much we might sometimes wish otherwise. It has its moments of sadness, as well as gladness. We must learn from the sadness and build on the gladness.'(xxvi)

When she visited Jallianwala Bagh, she showed her respects with a 30-second moment of silence. During the visit, she wore a dress described as pink apricot or saffron, which was of religious significance to the Sikhs. She removed her shoes while visiting the monument and laid a wreath at the monument (xxvii).

In February 2013 David Cameron became the first serving British Prime Minister to visit the site. He laid a wreath at the memorial, and described the Amritsar massacre as 'a deeply shameful event in British history, one that Winston Churchill rightly described at that time as monstrous. We must never forget what happened here and we must ensure that the UK stands up for the right of peaceful protests.'(xxviii)

The tragic event has also featured in various books and films, including Salman Rushdie's novel *Midnight's Children,* Richard Attenborough's film *Gandhi* and in *The Jewel in the Crown,* a Television series, recounted by the fictional widow of a British officer who is haunted by the inhumanity of it and tells how she came to be reviled because she defied the honours to Dyer and instead donated money to the Indian victims.

The 1930s were a time of much political activity in India, but the Sikhs had little influence on events, although they were increasingly alarmed at the Muslim League's demand for a separate Muslim state. The more so, because the Sikh homeland was in the middle of the proposed Pakistan. As a front page headline in *The Statesman* made clear, 'The Sikhs will under no circumstances accept Pakistan.'

Not only were the Sikhs' protests disregarded: their very existence was ignored when the boundaries of the new India and Pakistan were hurriedly drawn up by Sir Cyril Radcliffe, a British jurist, who had never before been to India. He arrived in India on July 8th. He completed his division of the country, based on the areas in which Hindus or Muslims were dominant, on August 13th. It was implemented on August 15th.

Even before Independence, many Sikhs had been massacred and partition was followed by the slaughter of thousands more, as well as of many Hindus and Muslims. It is reckoned that some ten million people were displaced and well over a million butchered to death.

In the region of Punjab, massacre on the basis of religion, became everyday news. Before partition thirty five per cent of the population were either Hindus or Sikhs. Within a few days of partition the figure was almost zero. There was also violence in Delhi. The sheer number of victims may blind us to the reality of the suffering of individuals. Let this one, of many horror stories, remind us of the anguish of each of the million or more people who were massacred.

'I am originally from Thoha Khalsa; I was 16-years-old in 1947. We were living peacefully in the village. People were very friendly and co-operative. Sikhs were rich people, as they ran the shops and had thriving businesses. They often helped us on money matters. I often used to visit Darshan Singh's house. On the evening of March 6, Muslim mobs from the surrounding villages entered Thoha Khalsa and gave ultimatums to the Sikhs to convert. On that evening, the impact of their presence was negligible due to the lateness of the hour but the actual clashes started the next morning, when their numbers swelled to some thousands. After resisting for three days, the Sikhs hoisted white flags from their *havelis*. They had only acted in self-defence.

But when defeat and dishonour was imminent, Sikh men started killing their own women. I still remember when Bhansa Singh killed his wife with tears in his eyes. They all gathered in the central *haveli* of Sant Gulab Singh. In the span of some hours, I witnessed the deaths of almost 25 women. It was such a horrible scene. For six days, the whole village witnessed orchestrated looting and killing. While their men fought, the Sikh women started gathering near a well around the garden. It was almost after noon, and I watched from nearby with two of my friends. Some of the women held their children in their arms. They sobbed desperately as they jumped into the well. In about half an hour, the well was full of bodies. I went closer and realised that those who were on top were trying to submerge their heads. No space remained. A few came up and jumped again.

It was a terrible scene. They were determined to die rather than sacrifice their honour. In one week, all the remaining Sikhs and Hindus were compelled to leave their native place' (xxiv)

12. Sikhs in the New India

Violence not only marked the departure of the British, but soon spread across newly independent India. Thousands of displaced Hindus and Sikhs arrived in India and rekindled latent Hindu-Muslim hostility. In September 1947, ethnic violence erupted on a terrifying scale in Delhi. Mainly it was a Hindu-Muslim conflict; but it endangered all minorities.

Despite the unrest, the government with its Five Year plans set about tackling some of the major problems that faced the new state. The first Five Year Plan, because of India's history of recurrent famines, made 'self-sufficiency' a priority. In this, the Punjab had a crucial role. Government investment in irrigation and rural development, the introduction of high-yielding varieties of seeds and the increased use of chemical fertilizers, - 'the Green Revolution - and as well as the skill of the Sikh peasantry, soon made the Punjab the 'bread-basket' of India. Its wheat output rose from about 1 million (metric) tons in 1950 to over 11 million by 1990 and there was a similar rapid increase in rice and cotton.

Even so, no major state-sponsored industrial development was situated in the Punjab. The government said it was because they did not want to site such development too near to the border with Pakistan – but some Sikhs felt they were being discriminated against. In the long term this may have been a blessing, as it avoided environmental damage to the state's prosperous agriculture. Moreover, many small and medium industries grew up and by 1990 employed well over half the population.

The growing feeling that the Punjab was being marginalised by the government in New Delhi increased sharply after two new Hindi-speaking states, Harayana and Himachal Pradesh, were carved out of the Punjab. In addition, Chandigar, which was designed by Le Corbusier, an at the time ws as the capital of the Punjab, was made Union Territory. It is now the capital of two states, Haryana and Punjab. As union territory, the city is governed directly by the Union Government.

Moreover as the boundaries of states were being redrawn on the basis of language, why was the Punjab almost the last in the queue? Indira

Gandhi, probably, felt such action would let down the Congress Party's Hindu supporters in the area. The media, maybe, with encouragement from the government, implied that the demand for a Punjabi speaking state was in fact a demand for a separate Sikh state, and that this would stir up tension between the Hindu and Sikh communities. Indeed the creation of linguistic states is now seen to have increased communalism, which was defined on a religious basis.

In the early 1970s, the largest political party, the Alkali Dal, which had been secular in its approach, now became the defender of the Sikh community. It warned that the Sikh community and their faith were in danger. This move, however, weakened the Alkali Dal's political standing and the party was defeated in the 1972 provincial elections.

In 1975 political activity was suspended when Prime Minister Indira Gandhi unilaterally declared a state of emergency across the whole country. It lasted for twenty-one months from 1975 to 1977.

The Alkali party, led by Sant Harchand Singh Longowal, launched a 'Save Democracy' movement. Over 40,000 members of the party were jailed for their support of what was the most vigorous opposition to the emergency. Indira Gandhi never forgave the Alkalis for their resistance.

In March 1977, Mrs Gandhi called a snap general election, in which she was defeated. Soon afterwards, the Alkali party softened its emphasis on being the defender of Sikhism. In the Anandpur Resolution, it recognised that India 'is a federal and republican entity of different languages, religions and cultures.'(xlii) The Resolution called for a reform of the constitution on real and meaningful federal principles. This was misrepresented and attacked in the media because it would weaken national unity.

Indira Gandhi regained power in January 1980. Jarnail Singh Bhindranwale, a devout Sikh preacher and teacher, opposed Alkalis' support for co-existence as threat to Sikhism. In December 1983, Jarnail Singh Bhindranwale moved into the Golden Temple.

Soon afterwards, the Alkali leaders, angered by the Government's refusal to discuss any of their demands, symbolically burned a page of the Indian constitution.

The government and the media linked Bhindranwale and the Akali leaders and portrayed them both as extremists and a threat to national unity. This gave them a pretext in June 1984, to move troops and tanks into the Temple to expel Bhindranwale and his few supporters. The Akal Takht was destroyed and some five thousand Sikhs – mostly non-combatants were killed. This desecration of their most holy place shocked Sikhs around the world. It also helped Indira Gandhi win the next election by claiming that she had saved the nation for extreme Sikh 'secessionists.' Less than five months later, Indira Gandhi was dead – assassinated by two of her bodyguards, who were Sikhs.

Immediately hundreds of innocent, peace-loving Sikhs in Delhi and other North Indian cities were attacked and killed and properties looted. Government officials and the police did nothing to stop the attacks – some may have aided and abetted it. By the Government's own reckoning nearly three thousand people were killed or burnt alive in just four days – probably the number was over 6,000.

Soon afterwards, India suffered another devastating tragedy. The Bhopal disaster is considered the world's worst industrial disaster. It occurred on the night of 2–3 December 1984 at the Union Carbide India Limited (UCIL) pesticide plant in Bhopal, Madhya Pradesh. Over 500,000 people were exposed to methyl isocyanate (MIC) gas and other chemicals. The highly toxic substance made its way into and around the shanty towns located near the plant. Estimates vary on the death toll from about, 4,000 to 8,000, with half a million people injured.

Rajiv Gandhi, Indira Gandhi's son, quickly ordered an enquiry into the Bhopal disaster. Sikhs noted with disgust, there was no enquiry into the Delhi atrocities. A Citizen's Commission of five non-Sikhs, however, deplored 'the incredible and abysmal failure of the administration and the police; the instigation by dubious political elements; the equivocal role of the information media, and the inertia, apathy and indifference of the official machinery and other enquiries.'(xxv)

Rajiv Gandhi said of the riots, 'when a big tree falls, the earth shakes.' Newspapers and human rights groups claimed the massacre was organised. In 2011, Human Rights Watch reported the Government of India had 'yet to prosecute those responsible for the mass killings.' The collusion of political officials and the judiciary's failure to penalise the killers alienated normal Sikhs and increased support (although always a small minority) for an independent Sikh state of Khalistan.

The twenty-first century has, so far, been largely peaceful, although political debate in India is always vigorous. In 2015 there were protests after a copy of the Guru Granth Sahib was desecrated, but on this occasion India's Home Minister Rajnath Singh promised the Chief Minister of the Punjab 'all possible help' to restore peace in the state. Likewise the Akal Takht, the supreme temporal seat of Sikhs, the opposition Congress party and Sikh leaders all appealed for peace.

Sikhs have also played an increasingly important role in public life, as shown by the fact that Manmohan Singh, an economist and politician, who served as the Prime Minister of India from 2004 to 2014. He was the first Sikh to hold the office.

13. Sikhs in the Diaspora

Although the majority of Sikhs still live in India, there are now Sikh communities in many other countries. Of approximately 27 million Sikhs worldwide, just over 20 million live in India: but according to the 2011 census, they are just under 2% per cent of the total population. Out of that total, 77% are concentrated in the state of Punjab, which is the only Indian state where Sikhs are in the majority. Nearly 14% of the population of Chandigarh, (Union Territory) and over 5% of the population of Delhi are Sikhs (xxxi). In the rest of the world, the largest communities now are in the United States of America, Canada and Britain, with about half a million in the USA and rather less in both Canada and Britain. (xxvi)

Sikhs in Asia
The first Sikhs to leave India, however, were among the growing number of Indians, who as British rule spread in India, were exported, either as slaves or indentured labour to work in Fiji, Malaya, Africa and the West Indies. As the Punjab only became part of the Empire in the second half of the nineteenth century, the first shipping agencies in the Punjab date to eighteen eighties so the 'export' of Punjabis did not begin until the late nineteenth century.

Punjab's entry into the indenture system was problematic. Planters in the West Indies complained that Punjabi migrants 'refused to work in the fields, and nearly all have been unruly or troublesome.' In Fiji, too, it was noted that 'Sikhs are an unusual group: they are prepared to fight for their rights.' This was partly because many of them were 'soldiers or something of that sort.'

When C V Creagh, who was a British deputy superintendent of police in the Sind, was transferred to Hong Kong, he recommended that his trusty Sikh policemen from the Punjab should be recruited for the Colony's new police force. 100 Sikh migrants, therefore, arrived in Hong Kong in 1867 and soon more were recruited for Singapore. By the 1890s there were Sikh centres in Singapore, Penang in Malaysia and Taiping, in Southern China. By 1939, nearly half the Hong Kong police were Indians, most of whom were Sikhs: but in 1952, they were expelled and a number came to Britain. Malaya also recruited Sikhs and some went to New Zealand.

Sikhs in East Africa

The history of the Sikhs of East Africa begins in the 1890's, when the area was coming under British control, although detachments of Sikh Regiments had seen service in certain parts of East Africa in previous years. The Sikhs, who were brought from India to build the old Uganda Railways, were skilled workmen - carpenters, blacksmiths and masons. They came in dhows (sailing vessels) under considerable hardship. The Sikhs were quick to understand the specialised requirements of the Railways and many became fitters and turners and boiler-makers. The early settlers had to face marauding lions that were a constant threat to their lives. It is estimated that over 2,000 workers lost their lives in the building of the railway. Long before the motoring era, they also played an invaluable part, with the other Punjabis, in solving the transport problem of the country by building and operating Indian style bullock carts.

Soon the first arrivals were joined by more educated Sikhs, who either found management jobs in the railway or became policemen, and remained in the country for several years. Many, but not all, of the original Sikh workers returned to India. They were replaced and augmented by others who came of their own volition, tempted by the by the poster 'The Gateway to East Africa.'

The Uganda railway in fact started in Mombassa in Kenya, which had come under British control in 1887, and was the main port at which workers from India arrived. Many moved on and soon Nairobi, where the largest number of Sikhs now live, grew out of a railway camp into a township. The Sikhs who had settled there arranged for their families to join them.

Their standing received a considerable stimulus with the arrival, during World War I, of a large number of Sikh Troops from India, some of whom were officers. As Sikhs began to settle in their adopted countries a sense of community was imbued by the building of gurdwaras. As the community prospered it turned its attention to its youth. Several Khalsa schools, open to all faiths, were built. Medical facilities including hospitals, clinics and dispensaries, were established, also serving the wider community.

As African countries gained their independence, the situation of Sikhs and all Indians changed dramatically. Sikhs in Uganda were compelled to leave in 1972, although some have returned. Many of them came to the UK. Some Sikhs chose to leave Kenya, but there is a thriving community in Kericho, which I visited for a meeting of Global Co-operation for the Common Good, hosted by Bhai Sahib Mohinder Singh Ahluwalia, the third in line of Sikh spiritual leaders of Guru Nanak Nishkam Sewak Jatha (GNNSJ).

Compared to those Sikhs who came to Britain soon after the Second World War, Sikhs from East Africa were used to living as an expatriate community and took pride in wearing the traditional symbols of Sikhism. Their arrival strengthened the identity and the visibility of the British Sikhs as a whole.

Although there are now few Sikhs in the country, it was fitting that in 2014 the Uganda postal service commemorated 100 years of Sikhs settling in the country by issuing four special postage stamps. The four stamps depicted the gurdwara on Sikh Road, Kampala; the Khanda, the Nishan Sahib and the Golden Temple in Amritsar.

Sikhs in Canada

The first Sikhs to come to North America arrived in Vancouver in 1887. After parading in London for Queen Victoria's Golden Jubilee, a Sikh regiment travelled to British Columbia before returning home. So, although there are now more Sikhs in the USA, we shall tell the story of the Canadian Sikh community first. Census figures show that there were 455,000 Sikhs in Canada in 2011, double the 1991 population estimate of 145,000. Sikhs accounted for some five per cent of the 1.8 million new immigrants who came to Canada during the 1990s.

Today almost half of Canada's Sikh population lives in British Columbia, where the first Sikh immigrants, who arrived in 1904 established themselves. Soon, after their arrival, however, the Canadian Government took steps to restrict immigration. It decided that only people with a through ticket from their country to Canada would be allowed in. There was no direct service from India to Canada, so the number of new arrivals dropped dramatically and some of the Sikhs in Canada crossed the border to the USA.

In 1914, however, a Sikh business man in Hong Kong tried to get round the rule. He chartered an old boat called the 'Kamagata Maru' and collected 376 passengers from Hong Kong and Shanghai. After a horrendous journey, the emigrants – almost all of whom were Sikhs – reached Vancouver. But they were not allowed to land, shots were fired across the decks and requests for medical attention for those who were ill were refused. To add to their suffering, when the weary travellers returned to Calcutta they were greeted by police who ordered them on to a train to the Punjab, where they were interned. Many of the returned Sikhs resisted and other Sikhs protested. 19 Sikhs and four policemen, including two British officers, were killed.

Despite the hostility they faced, the small Sikh community in Canada quickly established religious institutions in British Columbia. Vancouver Khalsa Diwan Society was created in 1906 and it built the first permanent gurdwara two years later. By 1920, a few other gurdwaras had been established.

Canadian Sikh religious institutions reached another stage of development in the 1920s, when wives and children of legal Sikh residents were allowed entry to the country. The Sikh religion provided the basis for a strong collective identity between the World Wars. Very few Sikhs renounced the faith or married outside it, but second-generation men cut their hair and beards to conform to Canadian dress codes. Some women wore dresses instead of the traditional Punjabi suit, the salwar kameez.

Sikhism

Sikhism in Canada began to change its character in the 1950s as Immigration resumed. In the 1960s and 1970s, tens of thousands of skilled Sikhs, some highly educated, settled across Canada, especially in the urban corridor from Toronto to Windsor. As their numbers grew, Sikhs established temporary gurdwaras in every major city east of Montreal. These were followed in many instances by permanent *gurdwaras* and Sikh centres. Most cities now have several gurdwaras, each reflecting slightly different religious views, social or political opinions, or caste backgrounds. At most of them there are Sunday services, usually followed by langar.

True to the tradition, services are open to anyone who obeys the conventions for entering a temple: namely - removal of footwear, head covering, and refraining from smoking or drinking. Although a few Canadian congregations have chairs and tables, for the most part worshippers sit on carpets, with men and women sitting on separate sides of the room.

Gurdwara observances are also held to celebrate the various Gurus and traditional celebrations such as Baisakhi Day. Weddings, some of which are still arranged by parents, are held in the gurdwara, or a hotel, or in a family home. Many parents, either at home or at the gurdwara, teach their children about their religion and language. Some second-generation Sikhs speak Punjabi from an early age but must be formally taught the unique Sikh *gurmukhi* written script in order to read from the *Guru Granth Sahib*. Sikh Canadians who visit India often go on a pilgrimage to the famous Sikh shrines, especially the Golden Temple.

Canada has a good reputation for communal harmony, as I have seen on visits to Vancouver, where there are a number of multi-faith associations. Events in India, however, have caused difficulties. During the 1984 attack on the Golden Temple, some Sikhs in Canada held demonstrations against the Indian government. This caused a deterioration of relations between Canadian Sikhs and Canadian Hindus, which were further strained when Indian Prime Minister Indira Gandhi was assassinated by two of her Sikh security guards in October 1984. On 23 June 1985, Air India Flight 182 was blown up, in what was widely regarded as an act of revenge against the government of India. Many of the 329 victims were Sikhs.

Several provincial court cases have heard arguments regarding the issue of security versus religious freedom stemming from orthodox Sikh students who wear a *kirpan* while in school. In 2002, the Quebec Superior Court ruled that a 12 year-old student named Gurbaj Singh Multani had the right to wear the *kirpan* at school, provided it was sheathed and concealed under his clothes. In 2004, the Québec Court of Appeal struck down the decision, ruling that community safety was more important than Multani's religious freedom, and that the ceremonial dagger violated the 'weapons and dangerous objects' of the student conduct code. However, in 2006 the Supreme Court decided that religious tolerance was to be encouraged in Canadian society and that a total ban infringed the guarantee of religious freedom under the Charter of Rights and Freedoms. Several provinces have addressed the issue by limiting the blade size or requiring that the *kirpan* be hidden under clothing. Sikh MPs may wear a *kirpan* in the Canadian Parliament, but they are still banned from some courtrooms and Transport Canada bans all 'knives or knife-like objects.' Heightened Sikh consciousness has led to an increase in the number of Canadian Sikhs who belong to the Khalsa.

Sikhs in the USA

There are today about 600,000 Sikhs in the USA. The first Sikhs to arrive in the USA were those who crossed the border from Canada. As all immigrants from India, many of whom were from the Punjab, were at that time, labelled as 'Hindoo', it is hard to know how many were Sikhs. It is estimated that 7,348 Asian Indians migrated to the United States and Canada between 1899 and 1920. (xxxiii).

As immigration restrictions tightened in Canada, more immigrants came directly to California. They mostly passed through the Angel Island station, in San Francisco Bay, which was the point of entry for those coming across the Pacific - less well known than Ellis Island, which processed immigrants crossing the Atlantic. Some immigrants had served in the British Indian Army and were used to the way authority and institutions worked in the Western world. Others who came as labourers looking for railroad, lumber, or agricultural jobs, were often known as 'Hindu crews' and had to face considerable

prejudice, being viewed as strange and oddly dressed. Between 1903–1908 two thousand Punjabis worked on the Western Pacific Railways in Northern California. They also worked on a 700-mile road between Oakland and Salt Lake City. In time, others took up farming in the Sacramento Valley, San Joaquin Valley and in the Imperial Valley in California. At first it was largely single men who came to make money to send home.

All too soon native Californians expressed opposition to further immigration and some homes were attacked. In 1920 a government report indicated that since 1910, the number of Asian Indians in the United States had increased by 33.5% and were seen as an economic threat by American farmers. As a result, immigrants were barred from owning and leasing land, and no further immigrants were allowed in.

One of the ways that Sikhs attempted to fight discrimination was by challenging American immigration and citizenship laws in court. A famous case involved Bhagat Singh Thind, who came to the USA in 1913 to pursue higher education in an American university. He had served in the British Indian army and was recruited by the US Army in July 1918, to fight in World War I. A few months later, he was promoted to the rank of an Acting Sergeant. He received an honourable discharge in late December 1918, with his character designated as 'excellent.'

After the war he sought the right to become a naturalized citizen, following a legal ruling that Caucasians had access to such rights. (At the time, Indians were categorized as Caucasian by anthropologists). So Thind took the citizenship oath and received his certificate in the state of Washington on December 9, 1918. He was wearing his military uniform, as he was still serving in the army. Only a few days later, his citizenship was revoked on the grounds that he was not a white man. Thind applied for citizenship again in the neighbouring state of Oregon in 1919. A Federal judge heard testimony from the Immigration and Naturalization Service (INS) and ruled in favour of Thind. He became a citizen in November of 1920. The INS appealed the decision and the case was sent to the Supreme Court, which retroactively denied all Indian

Americans citizenship for not being Caucasian in *'the common man's understanding of the term.'*(xxxiv). Finally in 1935, the 74th congress passed a law allowing citizenship to USA veterans of World War I, even those from the 'barred zones.' Thind received his USA citizenship through the state of New York in 1936, taking the oath for the third time to become an American citizen.

Another way that some Sikhs evaded the ban was to marry Hispanic women, who were allowed to own land: but it was soon ruled that any American female citizen, who married 'an alien ineligible to citizenship,' would lose her citizenship and become ineligible for land rights. Then land was transferred to their children, who, thanks to the Fourteenth Amendment were legally, American citizens.

Despite the unfriendly environment, Sikhs constructed places of worship where they could build fellowship and community life. These Gurdwaras also provided shelter, food, and help to all immigrants of whatever caste, creed, or religion.

The virtual exclusion of Asian Indians since the "Barred-Zone" Act of 1917 ended on July 2, 1946 with the passage of the Luce-Celler Bill, which granted natives of India the right to American citizenship and an annual naturalization quota of one hundred. (This was gradually increased). Some Sikhs already in the USA quickly arranged for their families to join them. Of those coming from India in the fifties a great number were Sikhs but by the eighties only about 5% of immigrants from India were Sikhs. California, where two Gurdwaras had been opened in 1948 remained the favourite place to settle.

In 1956 Dalip Singh Saund became the first Asian American to be elected to the USA Congress. He had come to the USA in the 1920s to study at the University of California at Berkeley where he eventually earned a Ph.D. in mathematics. He managed a farm in California and worked for the right of Asian Indians to become citizens. He served for two terms.

The Immigration Act of 1965 gave preference to highly educated professionals whose skills were needed in the USA. Thus the Sikhs entering the country after 1965 differed greatly from most of their predecessors. The Sikh community increased fourfold between 1965–75. By 1975, more than 8,000 Sikhs had become American citizens.

New Sikh communities quickly organised gurdwaras: meeting in one another's homes or renting space for festivals and programmes. Gradually they found an appropriate building or site for a new building. In Yuba City, California, the gurdwara, which was opened in 1969, built by progressive Sikhs, was equipped with folding chairs and seated 2,000 people in the main hall. Soon, however newer more traditional immigrants insisted on the removal of the chairs. In Los Angeles, the Sikh Study Circle, opened the doors of city's first gurdwara in 1969 to celebrate the 500th birthday of Guru Nanak.

In America, as elsewhere, the attack on the Golden Temple in 1984 created shock waves. Sikhs in the USA were outraged, and protested publicly. In the same year the World Sikh Organization was established to protect the social, political, religious and human rights of Sikhs. The newspaper, *World Sikh News*, based in Stockton, California was started. By the mid-1980s, also, conferences co-sponsored by the Sikh community were held at several universities.

Various nation-wide organizations link Sikhs to each other and Sikhs also play an important part in interfaith activities, including the North American Interfaith Network and the Parliament of World Religions.

There have also been new developments, most notably 3HO, the 'Healthy, Happy, Holy Organization,' which was founded in the USA by Yogi Bhajan (1929-2004) in 1971. The movement's roots are in the Radhasoami Satsang founded in Agra by Swami Shi Dayal in 1861. Yogi Bhajan came to the USA in 1969. Breaking the centuries old tradition of secrecy surrounding the empowering science of Kundalini Yoga, he began teaching publicly and gave the, soon to be called, "Baby Boomers" an effective alternative to the prevalent drug culture. I have to admit when I was invited to join a gathering of 3HO, I wondered whether or not it was a Sikh gathering but was immediately impressed by the spirit of devotion and the inspiring personality of Yogi Bhajan.

The movement has spread across America and internationally. Yogi Bhajan made an important contribution to the Sikh life in the USA and met leaders of other faiths. His motto was 'If you can't see God in all, you can't see God at all.'

There have been problems with the host community. The wearing of the *kirpan*, or short sword, often alarms security forces. I recall that at a big interfaith service in the Cathedral in San Francisco held to mark the sixtieth anniversary of the signing of the United Nations Charter, one Sikh student was not allowed in because he was wearing a *kirpan*. My wife and I with others explained to the officers the significance of the sword and eventually he was admitted. Indeed already in 1994 the USA Court of Appeals had said that children could wear the *kirpan*.

Turbans have also been a problem. As elsewhere, Sikhs had to struggle to be allowed to wear turbans at work, especially in the police or public transport. The New York Police Department, after a lawsuit, allowed Sikhs to wear turbans and keep their uncut hair and beards. In 2007, however, the Transportation Security Administration mandated that Sikh turbans would be subject to additional security screening, including possible removal and/or pat-down of the turban at security checkpoints.

At the same time, Sikhs were playing a fuller part in the life of the nation. In 2009, despite the army's ban on 'conspicuous religious articles,' two Sikhs - an emergency medicine doctor and a dentist - became the first Sikhs to enlist in the USA Army. Then in 2012 the Washington, D.C. police force voluntarily allowed Sikh police officers to keep their articles of faith, including beards and turbans. The policy announcement came after an eight year partnership between the Washington D.C. police force and the Sikh American Legal Defense and Education Fund. The Metropolitan Transit Authority of New York City now allows all religious headwear, such as turbans and veils, provided they are blue to match the MTA uniforms.

Yet, as in other countries, parallel to the growing process of integration, immigrants have faced prejudice and active hostility. During the First Gulf War, Sikhs, with their turbans and beards, mistaken by some Americans for Muslims, were sometimes harassed.

There were attacks on some Sikh gurdwaras, which were defaced with graffiti.

Their problems were even greater after the horror of 9/11. Many turban-wearing Sikh men and boys were targeted because they 'looked like terrorists.' On September 15th, 2001, Balbir Singh Sodhi, a Sikh immigrant from the Punjab, was shot and killed outside a petrol station in Mesa, Arizona. Very quickly, the Senate unanimously passed a Resolution on Hate Crimes against Sikh-Americans.

Then in August 2012, six Sikh worshippers were killed at a gurdwara in Oak Creek, Wisconsin. The shooting was labelled a hate crime after it was found out that the gunman, who was also killed, had ties to white supremacist groups. In the following weeks Sikhs and non-Sikhs alike gathered in gurdwaras, churches, and community centres, around the nation, to remember the slain and to stand up against intolerance. The 2016 Presidential election campaign was in some places marked by greater hostility. *Time Magazine* reported that 'In the days since the presidential election, across the country, there have been more incidents of racist or anti-Semitic vandalism and violence.'(xxxv)

14. Sikhs in the United Kingdom

The United Kingdom (UK), after Canada and the USA, is the country with the next largest Sikh population. It numbers rather under half a million people – mostly in England.

In 1854, Dalip Singh, the last ruler of the Sikh Empire, as we have seen, was exiled to Britain to live as a lonely member of the royal aristocracy. For much of the time his home was an estate in Suffolk. He died in 1893. In the early years of the twentieth century some Sikh princes and students spent a time in Britain but did not settle in the country. In the 1930s a few Sikhs from villages in the Punjab as well as Muslims settled in the Midlands or the North. They were mostly unskilled labourers. The only permanent Gurdwara in Britain for the first half of the 20th Century was established in 1911 in Putney (moving to Shepherd's Bush in 1913) following a generous donation by Maharaja Bhupinder Singh, the King of Patiala, and the Gurdwara became the first port of call of all Sikhs during that time.

Immigration, on a large scale, only started after the Second World War and the horrors of the Partition of India. In the 1950's, British firms started recruiting labourers from overseas. It is said that the Sikh population of Southall in West London grew to be the one of the biggest in the West in the 1950s because the recruitment officer of a newly opened rubber factory in the area had worked as an Army Officer in British India. He wanted to offer jobs to Punjabis whom knew to be hard-working. Some Sikhs, often ex-service men, persuaded by the voucher scheme, hoped to rebuild their lives by working for a time in the UK. Hopes of making a quick fortune returning home and then returning home quickly faded. Instead they arranged for their families to join them and settle in Britain. The number of Sikhs coming to Britain both from India and East Africa peaked in the late 1960's. Many of those who came from East Africa after the expulsion of Asians from Uganda by Idi Amin were professionals. By 2000, just about half the Sikhs had been born in Britain and now some 90% of Sikhs, who are under twenty, were born in the UK.

At that time, we were living in the Medway Towns and got to know some of the local Sikh community. When a colleague of mine, Revd Peter Absolom, and I discovered that the only place they could find to meet for prayer was the back room of a pub – most Sikhs are teetotallers – we offered them the use of a church hall. As there was already some debate among Christians whether church property could be used by members of another religion and whether redundant churches could be sold for use by members of other religions, we wrote a letter, published in *The Times*, explaining and justifying what we had done. We also started a local branch of the World Congress of Faiths, in which some Sikhs took part. I remember taking a group to visit the Gurdwara in Gravesend. We also offered a refugee family from Uganda the use of the vicarage, which, at the time, was empty.

Immigrants everywhere have divided pressures: to feel at home in a new society and to keep links with family and the traditions of the countries from which they come. After finding work and somewhere to live, learning the language is important, although many Sikhs spoke English and were well versed in English history and literature

Most Sikhs are proud of their faith identity but think of themselves as British. Many object to being labelled 'Indian' or 'Asian.' British courts recognise and protect Sikhs and Jews as separate racial groups. Even so, many Sikhs have experienced discrimination. Nearly one in five persons has encountered discrimination in a public place, such as a store, airport, or sporting venue. Sadly, with the growing fear of terrorist attacks, discrimination or hostility has become more common. The turban and kirpan appear to be the key triggers. Younger members of the community suffer the highest levels of discrimination as they have the greatest interaction in with British society.

Sexual grooming is another worry. Quite a large number of Sikh women have been targeted by grooming gangs or know a friend or relative who has been a victim or a target for sexual grooming. They also object to attempts to convert them, but take an active role in interfaith groups.

Many Sikhs own their own homes. Their unemployment rate is below the national average. In the 2011 Census, Jews and Sikhs had the

highest percentage of people in the 'managers, directors and senior officials' category. In 2017 General Election Sikhs had the highest turnout of any group. For the first time a turban-wearing Sikh, Tanmanjeet Singh Dhesei and a Sikh woman, Preet Kaur Gill, were elected to Parliament. Sikhs also donate six times more to charities than the average person in the UK, giving to national charities as well as supporting Gurdwaras and Sikh-based voluntary activity. Many Sikhs also regularly send money to family members still in India. It is not only money that links Sikhs in the UK to Sikhs in India. Many return for holidays to visit their families and perhaps to look for a bride or bridegroom. They also take a close interest in Indian politics. Sikhs from Britain also play a significant part in World Sikh international bodies.

The strongest link is the shared faith. Many cities now have purpose-built Gurdwaras, which serve as social as well as religious centres. Some of them are large and beautiful buildings. Religious leaders from India come to encourage the faithful. Some of the first settlers made concessions, such as having chairs in a Gurdwara or cutting their hair, but a more settled community has the confidence to maintain traditional practices, although chairs are usually provided for those with disabilities.

There is also cultural exchange. Some British cinemas show films in various Indian languages. A film about Dalip Singh – 'Black Prince' – was made in English in Hollywood and a film about Guru Nanak – 'Guru Nanak Shah Fakir'm' has English subtitles. Singers from the sub-continent often come to perform in the UK. Increasingly the host community welcomes the enrichment that Sikhs bring to life in the U.K. Lord Indarjit Sing's contributions to the BBC's 'Thought for the Day' are widely appreciated. Indeed, Gareth Johnson, Conservative M.P. for Dartford, has said that 'British Sikhs are the best example of cultural integration.'

15. Sikh Theology

God

As Sikh belief is derived from the Guru Granth Sahib and the lives and teachings of the Gurus, much of it will already be familiar. Nonetheless, an overall summary may be helpful. Indeed one brief summary is 'Always remembering God; earning one's livelihood through honest means; and sharing the fruits of one's labour with other people.'(xxxvi)

Theology is the attempt to systematise the teachings of a religion. The great Muslim theologian Al Ghazalia said, 'the aim of theology is merely to preserve the creed of orthodoxy and to defend it against the deviation of heretics.'(xxxviii) It is also an attempt to apply the faith in an ever changing world.

At the heart of Sikhism is belief in God, who reveals God's self to the devotee, although God is never fully comprehended by human beings. 'To the true and the true prophet alone is God's Light revealed with perfect clarity.'(xxxix). By meditation and a virtuous life, the faithful grow closer to God. Sikhism insists on the Oneness of God from whom all that is takes its being. The opening verse of the Adi Granth and the Japji describe God as Self Existent.

'The One Lord is the cause of all causes,
Knowledge, wisdom, discrimination are His gifts to us;
He is not far, He is not near, He is with us all...
Praise the Lord with abiding love.' (235)

Thou art O Lord art Self Existent and abiding in glory,
Ever united with everyone. (199)

As there is only One God – it is the One God whom all people worship, although they mistakenly give God different names and think theirs is the only God.

'There is but ONE God, but Hindus and Muslims think that their god is different from the god of other religions. The ONE God whom I worship is both Allah and Rama: to the formless one I bow my heart. Thus have I settled the dispute between Hindus and Muslims.' (1136)

With the insistence that God is one and without form, Sikhism rejects idolatry. Rather like some passages in the Hebrew Bible, the idea of worshipping a stone is mocked.

'You trample one piece of stone under your feet, and then worship a god made of the same stone. If the idol is god, the other stone must also be god.' (525)

All worship and adoration of idols end in nothing.' (1160)

There is similar mockery of idols in the Bible, in the Book of Isaiah,
The carpenter kindles a fire and bakes bread. He also fashions a god and worships it… No-one stops to think… "Half of it I used for fuel, I even baked bread over its coals, I roasted meat and I ate.
Shall I make a detestable thing from what is left? Shall I bow down to a block of wood? (44, 15-17)

The idea of incarnation is also rejected. No human being or avatar can be equated with God. 'Burned be the tongue which says God came to earth as a human being'(xl). The Gurus also rejected any attempt to worship them. God transcends the universe: but is also the Creator. The word *Nirankar*, (the Formless One) is used of God's transcendence and *Omkar* is used of God as the ground of Creation. The word *Nam*, (Name of God) is most often used of God's self-manifestation.

How can Nam be known? Nam is within us,
yet how can God be reached?
Nam is everywhere at work,
permeating the whole of space.
The perfect awakens you to the vision of Nam.
It is by the grace of God that one comes to enlightenment.' (1242)

Moses also when he asked God's name, received the mysterious reply, 'I AM WHO I AM.' (Exodus, 3, 14) The Psalms also often speaking of praising 'the Name of the Lord.' (Psalm 113, 3)

Sikhism

Sikhism insists on the transcendence of God and rejects pantheism, although God is omnipresent.
God is Primal Light and Eternal Being Creator of all the worlds (Jap 83).
God is the Essence of all religions. His is the Spirit that pervades all,
He is the glory of all, He is the Light of all. (Jap 113)

Guru Gobind Singh said,
Before God hears the loud trumpeting roar of an elephant, the cry of an ant reaches Him. In my folly, I thought Thou wert far off, but no deed I do, can ever be out of Thy sight. Thou who art All-seeing, all things Thou seest.

Sikhism not only emphasises the greatness of God it also affirms that he is close to all creatures. God loves all people and like a mother embraces her children. Bhai Gurdas (a contemporary of the early Gurus) said that 'If a person goes one step towards God, the Lord comes a thousand steps towards him.' God's love is unfailing and all human love is rooted in the Divine Love.

The Cherisher Lord is merciful and wise
He is compassionate to all.'(249)
The Lord is kind and compassionate to all beings and creatures;
His Protecting Hand is over all' (300)

O Guru Nanak, God has been kind and compassionate;
He has blessed me.
Removing pain and poverty,
He has blended me with Himself.' (315)

Only with His Will can pain, poverty, disease and hardships be
removed...God is everywhere.
On knowing the self,
A person meets God.' (1140)

God meets him Who realises his self
By the light shedding love of the. (364)

The Role of the Guru

The word 'Guru' is widely used in India of a teacher of spiritual wisdom. In Sikhism the word 'Guru' has a much more restricted meaning. It is used only of the ten Gurus and also of the Guru Granth Sahib. The Sat or true teacher is God, but the term is also used of the humans who embody the spiritual light of the Divine. The ten Gurus of Sikhism are not regarded as incarnations. Guru Gobind Singh said,

Those who call me God, will fall into the pit of hell.
Regard me as a humble servant of the Lord and have no doubt about it.
(Guru Gobind Singh *Bachiter Natak*, adh 6)

One commentator explains, 'He said this to 'stop Sikhs worshipping the Guru, instead of worshipping the Divine Light in the Guru.
In the true Guru He has installed His own Spirit.
Through Him, God reveals Himself'   (Asa di Var*)

The True reveals the Truth,
It is a wealth which is priceless.' (1092)

The One Eternal light resideth in the body,
The perfect and true reveals itself through the Word.' (125)

In St John's Gospel, Jesus says, 'I am the Light of the World' and St John says of Jesus that in him, the Word, which was with God from the beginning, became flesh (John, 8, 12 and 1, verses 1-4).

Sikhism too gives great attention to the Word (*Sabad*). Sabad is the all-pervading principle of the transcendent God, which is the active principle of creation. Sabad is also the mystic personality of the Guru. When one yogi asked Guru Nanak who was his Guru, he replied, 'The Word (Sabad) is my Guru.' In one of Guru Nanak's verses, the Word is personified and says,

With the beginning of the breath of life,
My system began also;
Its source is the Wisdom of the true.

The true is the Word (Sabad)
And human consciousness is the disciple.
What keepeth me in my detachment
Is meditating on the Ungraspable One,
Through the one Divine Word. (44)

In the Book of Proverbs in the Bible, Wisdom is also personified:
I was appointed from eternity, from the beginning, before the world
began… Whoever finds me finds life and receives favour from the Lord.
(Proverbs 8, 3 and and 8, 35)

There may be some meeting point between Sikh's understanding of the divine presence in the Guru and Liberal Christians' Christology, especially as the Gurus' objection was to the Hindu belief in avatars.

Merely seeing the Guru, is not enough – understanding the Guru's word is essential. Unlike *Darsana* (homage) in Hinduism, which may be paid to a holy image or person, in Sikhism *Darsana* is paid to the Guru Granth Sahib by listening to its words - not so much for instruction, but for meditation – rather like Taizé chants.

Karma

Sikhs believe in *karma* – the theory that we carry with us from previous lives the consequences of our good or bad behaviour; but our behaviour is not controlled by the past. Humans have free will, as some Sufis also said. Moreover, the burden of the past is lifted by the word of the Guru.

The Guru's word erases the blot of thousands of evil deeds of the past.
The greatest sinner can become the greatest saint. (1195)

Countless sins of the past are washed away
by the illumination of the Word.' (438)

The Gurus were well aware of the depth of human suffering. Guru Nanak said, 'The whole world is groaning in sorrow.' Sheikh Farid, in a verse included in the Guru Granth Sahib wrote,

I thought sorrow had engulfed me only,
But the whole world is engulfed in grief,
On looking at the world from the higher plane,
I found every home ablaze with sorrow's flames.'(945)

Heaven and hell are regarded as states of mind and not as eternal. Although karma is a punishment for bad behaviour, rebirth as a human is seen as a sign of God's compassion, because it gives a soul another opportunity to experience God's mercy.
'For many lives I have been separated from Thee, O Beloved:
My life is dedicated to Thee, and Thy Love.' (694)

This grace is available to everyone – whatever their status in life:
Guru Arjan said,
The chains are cut asunder, Rebirth has ended,
The mind is conquered and victory achieved.' (38)

Right Action and Service of Others

The definition of Sikhism quoted at the beginning of the chapter, besides urging followers 'always to remember God,' calls on them to earn their livelihood through honest means and to share the fruits of their labour with other people. Sikhism rejects extreme asceticism, as practised by Hindu sadhus. It sees the body not as a prison but as the temple of God,
In the body, God is present, The body is his temple,
In the body is a place of pilgrimage, Of which I am the pilgrim.(659)

Guru Nanak regarded householders (*Grihasthi*) as superior to Gurus. The house-holder, in Guru Nanak's teaching, is a person committed to moral duty, even if that involves suffering. Daily life should be governed by moral principles. He used the traditional Sanskrit term *Dharma* to imply not only experiences of the soul, but also pure and noble action. In the Japji he said, 'Human life is passed amidst the sequence of night and day, seasons and date: amidst all this play is fixed the earth – the theatre of righteous action.' All creation is holy:

Holy are the continents created by Thee, Holy thy universe,
Holy the worlds and forms therein.' (463)

This teaching is similar to that in this hymn by the Christian poet
George Herbert (1593-1633).
Teach me my God and King,
In all things Thee to see;
And what I do in anything
To do it as for thee.

Guru Nanak himself was married and had a family. After his extensive
travels, he settled for his last twenty years in Kartapur. He shared the
work of the community and saw nothing degrading in manual work,
unlike members of the Hindu higher castes. He said, 'they alone who
live by their own labour and share its fruit with others, have found the
right path.' Guru Nanak saw the world as the theatre of righteous
action. He stressed the importance of service or *Seva*. This was to be to
people of all castes, especially the lowest.
One who serves the higher castes, Is of great merit indeed.
But one who serves those of humble castes,
May indeed wear shoes made from my body.' (1256)

I have learnt by the light given by the perfect Master:
Recluse, hero, celibate or sannyasi,
None may expect to earn merit without devoted service
in which lies the essence of purity.' (992)

Only through devoted service in this world
May one find a place at the Divine Portal (26).

In a similar way, St Basil the Great asked someone who wanted to be a
hermit, 'Whose feet will you wash?'

Such service should to be all, regardless of caste or faith and even for
the enemy. This is illustrated in the well-known story of Bhai Kanhaiya,
who was often seen carrying a goatskin water pouch. He served water

to anyone who was thirsty, quenching the thirst of the dying and wounded soldiers. His acts of compassion, however, stirred up stern criticism amongst his fellow Sikhs. They complained to Guru Gobind Singh that Bhai Kanhaiya was even giving water to the fallen Hindu and Mughal attackers. They were especially annoyed because the city had been surrounded, stopping the supply of food and water.

Bhai Kanhaiya was called to the Guru, who asked him, 'These brave Sikhs are saying that you go and give water to the enemy and they recover to fight them again – Is this true?' Bhai Kanhaiya Ji replied 'Yes, my Guru, what they say is true. But Maharaj, I saw no Mughal or Sikh on the battlefield. I only saw human beings. Guru Ji, have you not taught us to treat all God's people as the same?'

The Guru was very pleased with the reply. He smiled and blessed Bhai Kanhaiya. Ji said, "Bhai Kanhaiya Ji, you are right, you have understood the true message of Gurbani". He then told the Sikhs who had complained that Bhai Kanhaiya had understood the deeper message of the Gurus' teachings correctly and that they all would have to strive to learn lessons from the priceless words of scripture (Gurbani). The Guru also gave Bhai Kanhaiya Ji some healing balm and said, 'From now on, you should also put this balm on the wounds of all who need it' (xxxviii)

Guru Gobind Singh reminded the Sikhs of Guru Arjan Dev's verse:
I have totally forgotten my self-centredness
Since I found the holy congregation.
No one is my enemy, and no one is a stranger.
I get along with everyone.
Whatever God does, I accept that as good.
This is the sublime wisdom
I obtained from the Holy One.
The One God is pervading in all (1229)

There are modern parallels: for example, Harman Singh, a Sikh from India, who was visiting New Zealand, broke religious protocol by removing his turban to help a six year old injured boy, who was bleeding profusely after being struck by a car, while he was walking towards his school. He was commended for his act of 'outstanding compassion and empathy.'(xxxix)

Similarly, Sarwan Singh was an Indian Sikh, who always wore his turban in public. When he saw a drowning dog, he realized that if he unfurled his turban, he might be able to loop it around the animal and save it. He did not hesitate to do so and saved the animal. (xl)

Again, there are parallels in the Bible in Jesus' picture of the Last Judgement.
'The King will put the sheep on his right and the goats on his left. Then the King will say to those on his right, "Come, you who are blessed by my Father; take your inheritance, the kingdom prepared for you since the creation of the world. For I was hungry and you gave me something to eat, I was thirsty and you gave me something to drink, I was a stranger and you invited me in, I needed clothes and you clothed me, I was sick and you looked after me, I was in prison and you came to visit me."

Then the righteous will answer him, "Lord, when did we see you hungry and feed you, or thirsty and give you something to drink? When did we see you a stranger and invite you in, or needing clothes and clothe you? When did we see you sick or in prison and go to visit you?" The King will reply, "Truly I tell you, whatever you did for one of the least of these brothers and sisters of mine, you did for me." (Matt, 25, 34-46)

Again, in his parable of the Good Samaritan, in answer to the question, "Who is my neighbour?" Jesus told the story of a man who was attacked by robbers. (Luke 10, 25-37

Two religious people saw him, but passed by on the other side of the road. It was a foreigner, a Samaritan, who helped him. Jesus then asked, "Which of these three do you think was a neighbour to the man who fell into the hands of robbers?" The lawyer replied, "The one who had mercy on him." Jesus told him, "Go and do likewise."

St Paul also said, *'If I give all I possess to the poor and surrender my body to the flames, but have not love, I gain nothing.'* (1 Corinthians 13, 3)

Christians and Sikhs agree on the supreme importance of love, which is rooted in God's love for every person and that 'true joy comes from forgiveness and truthful living.'

The Natural World: God's Creation.

Many Sikhs in the Punjab have earned their living by working on the land. By planting trees on waste land, growing flowers, fruit and vegetables wherever possible and by the conservation of water, as G.S Puri says, Sikhs transformed the Punjab into the 'breadbasket of India.'(xlvi)

Sikhs believe that God made human beings the guardians of the Natural World and today many Sikhs play a leading role in efforts to protect the Environment. Indeed the scriptures say that *'The Lord Himself is the Farm, Himself is the Farmer: Himself He Gaveth and Grindeth (the corn). Himself he cooketh, Himself He placeth it on the platter and Himself He eateth it too,* (550) The Guru Granth Sahib also quotes Kabir's reminder that *'the leaves too have life.'*(503). Conservation is seen as 'work for God.'

Although there is not room to give more examples, Sikh scholars and leaders are also actively concerned with many other contemporary issues, as the articles in leading Sikh journals bear witness.

16. Sikh Devotions

Sikh devotional life centres on the Gurdwara. Theologically speaking, for a Sikh the whole earth is a dharamsala — a place to practise dharma. The origin of the dharamsala can be traced back to the times of Guru Nanak. It was where the early Sikhs used to meet for worship and devotion. Sikh sources show that during Guru Nanak's travels, quite a few people felt attracted to his faith. Wherever he found his disciples, he both organised them into congregational circles (*sangats*), and encouraged them to build a religious centre. Still today when Sikhs settle in a new part of the world, as we have seen, they create a gurdwara, even if it is only a room in an ordinary house. Very soon, money is given for a beautiful purpose-built gurdwara.

Bhai Gurdas, an early Sikh scholar, says of its origin: 'Wherever Guru Nanak visited, that place became a place of worship. The most important centres, including those of the yogis visited by the Guru, became spiritual centres. Even houses have been turned into dharamsalas where kirtan (devotional singing) was sung on the eve of Vaisakhi (the Spring Festival).'

When he settled at Kartarpur, Guru Nanak built a dharamsala, although it is often called the first gurdwara. It was built on the banks of Ravi River in about 1521. It now lies about one mile across the border in Pakistan. The etymology of the word is from Guru and *dwara* (gateway) in Gurmukhi. Together the words mean 'the gateway through which the Guru could be reached.' Guru Hargobind, the sixth Sikh, introduced the word *gurdwara*. Following the death of Guru Gobind Singh, the Guru Granth Sahib became the Guru. So any building in which there is a copy of the Guru Granth Sahib is a Gurdwara, but many gurdwaras are splendid and ornate buildings.

The primary purpose of a Gurdwara is to be a place to praise God and to learn spiritual wisdom. It is also a centre for religious ceremonies. Children come there to learn the Sikh faith – its ethics, customs, traditions and texts. It is also a community centre, offering food, shelter, and companionship to those in need. It is managed by the community.

Inside the Gurdwara, the focus of attention, and the only object of reverence in the main hall (or *Darbar Sahib*) is the Guru Granth Sahib. It should always occupy the most exalted position. In a two storey house, the shrine room will be upstairs and if there is an attic it will be kept locked so that no one accidentally walks above the holy book. For the same reason, when in the evening the book is carried to a small quiet room for the night, it is carried on the head of the bearer and then carried in procession to the main hall at the start of the day's worship. I recall what a moving experience it was to be present very early in the morning at the Golden Temple, when the Guru Granth Sahib was brought in. In the main hall, the Guru Granth Sahib is placed on a raised platform (*Takht* and *Manji Sahib*, meaning "throne") under a canopy (*Chanani* or *Palki*), and covered with an expensive cloth when not being read. During a service a person waves a whisk or fan (*Chaur*) over the Guru Granth Sahib. The 'throne' is usually at the end of the hall, so that no one has their back to it, but far enough from the wall so that devotees and wedding couples can circumambulate it.

Although Sikhs show reverence to the Guru Granth Sahib, their reverence is to its spiritual content *(shabad)* not the book itself. The book is just the visible manifestation of the *shabad* or holy name of God. There are no statues or religious pictures in the *Darbar Sahib*, because Sikhs worship only God, and they regard God as having no physical form, although there will be pictures of the Gurus in other parts of the building. There are no candles, incense, or bells, although flowers are placed in front of the throne.

Like the Golden Temple, in some gurdwaras there are four doors: the Door of Peace, the Door of Livelihood, the Door of Learning and the Door of Grace. These doors are a symbol that people from all points of the compass are welcome. There is always a light on in a Gurdwara to show that the Guru's Light is always visible and is accessible to everyone at any time. Gurdwaras fly the Sikh flag outside, which is orange/yellow and has the Sikh emblem, 'Khanda' in the middle.

In India many Sikhs visit a Gurdwara before work. In Britain, some people do the same, but most Sikhs, who take their faith seriously, go at least once a week, and while Sikhs do not regard any particular day of the week as a holy day, they usually go to a Gurdwara on Sundays as this fits the pattern of life in Britain. Even more members of the community go there for festivals.

Anyone, of any faith, can visit a Gurdwara and will be made welcome. Before going into a Gurdwara, like Sikhs, they should remove their shoes and cover their heads before entering. It is forbidden to smoke or take tobacco onto the premises or to enter the Gurdwara while under the influence of alcohol or drugs.

On entering a Gurdwara, Sikhs will bow to the Guru Granth Sahib as the first thing they do, touching the floor with their forehead. This not only shows their respect but also indicates that they submit themselves to the truths contained in the book. Doing this at Amritsar, taught me a new respect for all holy books.

People also place an offering of food or money in front of the Guru Granth Sahib. This is used to run the Gurdwara and provide free food for the kitchen (*Langar*). The offering is not charity but a sharing of God's gifts. If a person has no money or food, they may offer flowers, or just some words of sincere thanks. Visitors should also bow and make an offering. After bowing, a Sikh will greet the congregation in a quiet voice with the words '*Waheguru Ji Ka Khalsa Waheguru Ji Ki Fateh* (The Khalsa owes allegiance to God, sovereignty belongs to God alone.)

In a Gurdwara, everyone sits on the floor on beautiful carpets. This is to be humble before the Guru Granth Sahib and it gives everyone a place of equal status to sit. Most people sit cross-legged with men and women usually on opposite sides. Cushions and seats are not usually allowed. No-one should sit with feet pointing at the Guru Granth Sahib. Anyone walking round the Guru Granth Sahib should do so clockwise. At the end of a service *karah prasad*, (a sweet that has been blessed) will be served. This should be taken and received in cupped hands as a gift from God.

Each Gurdwara has a *Granthi*, who organises the daily services and reads from the Guru Granth Sahib. A Granthi is not a priest but is the reader/custodian of the Adi Granth. Sikhs do not have ordained priests and any Sikh can lead the prayers and recite the scriptures to the congregation. A Granthi must be fluent in reading Gurmukhi and trained in all aspects of looking after the Guru Granth Sahib. They are expected to be faithful members of the Khalsa, with lives which exemplifies its ideals.

Sikhs do not have a general official liturgy that must be used in a Gurdwara, although there are rules for particular ceremonies. The morning service begins with the singing of *Asa Di Var*, a hymn written by Guru Nanak. Other hymns from the Guru Granth Sahib are then sung, accompanied by instruments. This hymn-singing is called *Kirtan* and is an essential part of Sikh worship. A sermon or talk, usually based on a theme from Sikh history, comes next. This is followed by the singing of *Anand Sahib*, a hymn written by Amar Das, the third Guru. The congregation then stands with eyes closed facing the Guru Granth Sahib for prayer (*Ardas*). During the prayer the word *Waheguru* (Punjabi for 'praise to Thee') is often repeated.

After the prayer, the Guru Granth Sahib is opened at a random page and the hymn found at the top of the left- hand page (*Vak* or *Hukam*) is read. The text is considered to be a relevant lesson for the day. Some people may do the same when they seek guidance. An example is that in 1920 there was an *amrit* ceremony at which many outcastes became Sikhs. When they made a pilgrimage to the Golden Temple, they were not offered *Prasad*. Some Sikhs protested, so the Guru Granth Sahib was consulted. The scriptures were opened at random. This is what the verse said,

'Upon the worthless, He bestows his grace, brother, if they will serve the True Guru. Exalted is the service of the True Guru, brother, to hold in remembrance the divine name. God himself offers grace and mystic union. We are meritless, transgressors, brother, yet the True Guru has drawn us to blissful union' (638)

The new converts were given *Prasad*.

On some special occasions, perhaps before a wedding or a festival, there may be a continuous reading (*akhand path*) of the Guru Granth Sahib by a relay of readers. The reading will last for about forty eight hours. Some Sikhs are critical of this, complaining that Sikhs are becoming blatant book worshippers, 'because the practice does not encourage an intelligent appreciation of the divine message.'

After a death, there will be regular readings of the scriptures at home. Sikhs will then usually bring the body to the gurdwara for family members and friends to pay their respects and for prayers around the open coffin. Following the cremation they return for further prayers, at which the *Sohilla,* an evening hymn in the Guru Granth Sahib, written by Guru Nanak is recited.

Music has been central to Sikh spiritual life since the founding of the community. In his own compositions, Guru Nanak called himself a minstrel, singing the divine message. He encouraged his Sikhs to sing the divine praises. Not only does the accompaniment of instruments to the singing of Sikh hymns heighten the aesthetic experience, but the Guru Granth Sahib is itself structured to the musical meters in which the Gurus composed their hymns.

Daily prayers have, for centuries, been a central part of the Sikh routine. The Gurus' compositions play a primary role in Sikh devotion from morning to night. Ideally before sunrise, Sikhs are supposed to wake up and recite Guru Nanak's *Jap-Ji*. Around sunset, they recite *Sodar,* also known as *Rahiras*, and then perform *Sohila* before sleeping. These three main prayers form the liturgy section at the very beginning of the Guru Granth Sahib. Guru Nanak's "Ballad in the Meter *Asa*" (*Asa Di Var*) is also a popular composition performed in the morning time, as are Amar Das' hymn *Anand* ("Bliss") and Guru Arjan's *Sukhmani* ("Pearl of Peace"). The practice of *ardas*, which is congregational supplication for the Lord of Creation's good graces, goes back to at least the 17th century. Sikhs usually end an *ardas* by asking divine grace for the community and "the welfare of all humanity" (*sarbat da bhala*).

Sikhs also practice meditation (*simran*), together or alone and contemplate the divine attributes. They may repeat a word like *Vahiguru* ("Great is the Guru ") to focus their attention. In Sikh theology, *shabad* ("the divine word") is both the content of divine revelation as understood by the individual, and the word of the Guru.

One of the culminating acts of a Sikh worship ceremony is the reading of the *hukam* ("command"), also known as *vak* ("utterance"). This is a slow reading of one complete hymn from a page opened at random by the reader, designated by the community, for all to hear and understand. If the congregational gathering is a court, then the *hukam* is the day's royal pronouncement from the Guru. After the reading of the *hukam*, a learned member of the community may be asked to offer commentary and clarification so that the members of the congregation can better enact that day's command from the Guru.

The *hukam* is to help people apply their faith in practice. The explanation (*katha*) of the *hukam* is also an important part of the process. Typically this explanation may be done by any competent member of the community. In English-speaking areas, a reading of an English translation of the *hukam* (or the projection of a digital English translation on a large screen) may accompany the reading.

The *hukam* from the central Sikh Gurdwara, the Darbar Sahib in Amritsar, is available on many Sikh television channels and the internet on a daily basis. The recitation of stories about Sikh history by highly- trained, celebrity performers is also readily available in the Diaspora. The ideal, however, is for local congregations themselves to perform, hear, and understand the Guru's word. Most important of all is for a Sikh to apply the teaching to his or her daily life.

Every Gurdwara has a Langar attached to it where food is served to anyone without charge. The term Langar is also used for the communal meal served at the Gurdwaras. The food served in the Langar must be simple, to prevent wealthy congregations turning it into a feast that shows off their superiority. Although Sikhs are not required to be vegetarian, only strictly vegetarian food is served in the Gurdwaras.

This ensures that any visitor to the Gurdwara, whatever the dietary restrictions of their faith, can eat in the Langar. The meal may include chapati, dal (pulses), vegetables and rice pudding.

Not only are members of every caste welcome, so also are guests of other faiths or people who would not otherwise have a hot meal. Memorably, at the Barcelona Parliament of World Religions, members of the Guru Nanak Nishkan Sewak Jatha, based in Birmingham, erected a great tent on the beach at which langar was offered to all participants. For some people, it was or most vivid memory of the gathering.

The Gurdwara provides educational programmes for children and people of all ages, as well as a wide range of other activities and meetings. Jjasjit Singh, however, suggests that many young Sikhs are more likely to learn about their faith from their parents or at special camps or from software translations: but they see the Gurdwara as 'safe-havens' in which they can simply 'be Sikh.'

17. Special Occasions

For many people it is at special occasions in life that a faith is at its most important. Some are joyful, such as a birth or a wedding, but also when a loved one dies many people look for comfort from their religion.

At Birth

In Sikh families, when a baby is born, a special prayer is read and a drop of *Amrit* (holy water with sugar) is placed on the baby's tongue. Then at a ceremony at the Gurdwara, the name of the baby is chosen. This is by opening the Guru Granth Sahib at random: the name must begin with the first letter of first word of the *Hukamnama* (the hymn chosen at random for the day) on the left hand side of the page. Singh ('Lion'), a reminder to be courageous, is added to boys' names while Kaur ('Princess'), to stress dignity, is added to girls' names.

For children there may be a ceremony called the *Dastaar Bandi* (wearing of the first turban). Boys and girls, are initiated into the Khalsa (community of faith) when they can read and recite prayers. Usually this is when they are aged between 14 and 16, although it can be earlier. *Amrit* is prepared in an iron bowl whilst the five special prayers (*Banis*) are recited by five Sikhs in the presence of the Guru Granth Sahib. During the ceremony the Amrit is blessed and sprinkled on the hair and eyes and a prayer is said. The ceremony is followed by a meal eaten together.

As members of the Khalsa, the young Sikhs will be expected to observe the five Ks: *Kesh,* uncut hair as a mark of holiness and submission to God's will; *Kangha*: a small wooden comb in the hair as a sign of cleanliness; *Kara*: a steel bracelet, a reminder that they are connected to God; *Kachhera*: short cotton underwear, more practical for daily life than the traditional *dhoti* worn in India; *Kirpan*: a sword, for protection.

Marriage

Sikhs should not get married until they are able to take on the responsibilities of married life. The word for a wedding *Anand Karaj* means 'blissful union.' Child marriage is forbidden. Sikh marriages may be arranged and assisted by parents but this is not necessary. In Western society more young people make their own choices.

A Sikh should not be concerned about the prospective spouse's caste. An engagement ceremony may take place before the wedding but this is not necessary. Any day suitable to the parties is fixed without regard to any superstition about auspicious days.

Most marriages take place in the morning. The ceremony starts with a meeting of the two sides called *Milni* at which *Shabads* (hymns) are sung. The couple sit side by side, facing the Guru Granth Sahib, with the bride on the left of the bridegroom. The couple and their parents (or guardians) stand up and a prayer is offered, seeking the Blessing of God at the commencement of the marriage. After the reading of the first stanza, the couple rises. To the accompaniment of music, they walk slowly round Guru Granth Sahib, the bridegroom leading the bride. The end of the sash which the bridegroom is wearing over his shoulder is placed by the bride's father, guardian or any other responsible person in the hands of the bride. Then, after a final prayer and reading, *prasad* is distributed to all present.

Any Sikh who has been initiated and practices the prescribed Sikh code in daily life can perform a marriage ceremony. This officiating person tells the couple of the duties of married life according to the Guru's teachings. He explains their mutual obligations as husband and wife. Sikh husband-wife love is modelled on the love between the human soul and the Supreme Soul as described in hymns composed by the Fourth Guru.

The bridegroom and bride vow faithfulness to each other in the presence of the Guru Granth Sahib and the holy congregation. They accept their obligations by bowing before the Guru Granth Sahib. The marriage is a holy rite and no document is necessary, although the legal requirements of the country of residence have to be met and in Britain many Gurdwaras have registrars to do this after the ceremony.

If a Sikh wants to marry a non-Sikh, he or she may meet opposition from their parents and also strong disapproval from the community., although whether it is completely forbidden seems to be disputed. (xliii)

In 1950, Sikh scholars and priests in India agreed on a code of conduct, after multiple attempts, to define what it meant to be a Sikh and what obligations should be placed on followers. It stated that the Sikh wedding ceremony (*Anand Karaj*) could only take place between two Sikhs of opposite sex.

Many Sikhs, therefore, consider this religious ceremony inappropriate if one partner is not a Sikh. Shamsher Singh, of the National Sikh Youth Federation, says 'They can have prayers inside the gurdwara, they can have part of the function inside a gurdwara, just not the religious ceremony. That's reserved for those of the Sikh faith.'

One web site, however, after insisting 'that the more a couple share, the happier they will be,' says Sikhism does not state that marrying out of the religion is wrong or a sin. 'Sikhism is a modern religion, which says that all humans are created equal. In no way Sikhism states that one should not marry another human because they are less human or inferior. Neither does Sikhism state not to marry anyone from another religion. All humans are equal but people from different religions do have different beliefs.' It adds, 'So, it is best to find someone who shares the same belief system so that you both learn and grow spiritually in the same path.'

Amandeep Madra, co-founder of the UK Punjab Heritage Association, says that, until recently 'Sikh traditions were highly pluralistic, with a willingness to learn and coexist with other concordant traditions. This is one of the most culturally appealing aspects of Sikhism in a modern, multi-cultural world. However, there has always been a more fearful voice that is threatened by the danger of being assimilated and indistinguishable from others.'

Sikhs in America seem fairly relaxed about the matter. In Britain, a few 'mixed marriages' have taken place. Recently, some Sikhs in Britain reacted angrily against a mixed marriage in a Gurdwara and forcibly interrupted the ceremony (xliv).

The Sikh Council, the largest body of British Sikhs, has ruled that temples should not hold mixed-faith weddings, but its advice is vague and calls for an end to protests. Yet sadly, in Sikhism, as in other faiths, religion can become a cause of division rather than promoting human unity. It is also not a theoretical matter, but one which can cause real pain.

Sikhs too cannot avoid questions about gay sex. The majority view is clearly one of disapproval but there is a website for Lesbian, Gay, Bisexual and Transgendered (LGBT) Sikhs, called SARBAT. The Guru Granth Sahib does not explicitly mention homosexuality. Giani Joginder Singh Vedanti, of the Akal Takht told visiting Sikh-Canadian MPs that they had a religious duty to oppose same-sex marriage, but they voted for it nonetheless (xliv).

Death

Sikhs, as we have seen believe in the cycle of life or reincarnation. The soul itself is not subject to death. Death is seen as only a journey back to God again. Because the soul never dies, it is expected that there will be no mourning when a Sikh dies. Instead funeral prayers are that the soul may be released from the bonds of reincarnation and become one with God. Devotional singing (*kirtan*) also brings comfort.

At the funeral Sikhs recite prayers, as the body is given a yogurt bath. Afterwards the body is dressed in new clothes, including the five symbols of Sikhism.

There then follows a small ceremony at a funeral home before the cremation. To start the service there is a community prayer. A minister may be present to offer prayers and say a few words, but this is optional. The two daily prayers - the Japji and Kirtan Sohila - are recited and the cremation begins. Hymns may be sung throughout the cremation. Sikhs, as we have seen believe in the cycle of life or reincarnation. The soul itself is not subject to death. Death is seen as a journey back to God again (xlvi).

18. Sikhism's Message for Today.

Advocates of interfaith fellowship are often accused of relativism and syncretism. Most religions claim that their message is true and Christians especially emphasize the uniqueness of Christ. Does gladly affirming God's presence in the teaching and practice of other faiths undermine that claim?

Studying together the teaching of the Gurus and the history of the Khalsa highlights the question of how to hold together particularity and universalism. Sikhs naturally are determined to defend their identity when it is threatened, as it has been in India and other countries where Sikhs now live.

It is, however, the universalism of the Gurus' message - that there is only One God whom people worship by different names - that speaks to the wider world. This is why Sikhs have made such an important contribution to the interfaith movement. Three examples will illustrate this.

Gobind Sadan

'You are just in time for prayers at the Jesus place' was the greeting we received when our World Congress group arrived at Gobind Sadan, a Sikh-based interfaith community on the edge of Delhi. A life-size image of Jesus stands in a garden at the place where Baba Virsa Singh, the founder of Gobind Sadan, had a mystical experience of Jesus' presence. As the sun sets, 125 candles are lit and the Lord's Prayer is recited in all the languages of those present.

Meanwhile other people sit in silent meditation around the sacred fire, known as *havan* in the ancient Vedic tradition of India. Butter (ghee), oil and incense are offered but there may not be a Hindu present. The place reflects the inner Light of God and those who spend time in prayer and meditation there say its healing light brings great peace.

At the same time, in the *Darbar Sahib* (Court of God) – the Guru Granth Sahib is being read. People from all backgrounds stand and waive the whisk (*chauri-sahib*) reverently over the 'Living 'Guru.

There are also shrines (*mandirs*) to the Hindu gods, Hanuman, Krishna, Shiva and Lord Rama and near the Jesus place, there is a small Mosque. Together these places and buildings are a visible model of the Sikh tradition, which not only honours all sacred paths, but recognises God's presence in each.

Gobind Sadan was founded by His Holiness Baba Virsa Singh. His family lived in a mud-brick village, where he helped on the farm. One day when he saw sap pouring out of the green fodder he had cut, he felt that he had committed a great sin and prayed that he would be released from that duty. At once, sores appeared on the soles of his feet—so painful that he could not work. From that time he began meditating regularly and was granted a vision of Baba Siri Chand, the elder son of Guru Nanak.(xlvi) There are many stories of the miracles that have followed prayers by Baba Virsa Singh.

Gobind Sadan was created as a place where his followers could dwell together and live out his teachings. There are now similar communities in the USA. Gobind Sadan, as I know from several visits, is a welcoming oasis of peace, but also at times there are large crowds for festivals or interfaith programmes.

Babaji makes no claim to be a Guru. Babaji continually says, 'God is the only Doer, the One who gives you everything. Give all your love to God.' He stresses that sectarian divisions have been created by humans, not by God or God's messengers. He also insists that 'religion is meant to be practical, 'not theoretical.' Like Guru Nanak, he encourages his followers to work hard to support themselves and share with others, whilst meditating on God. Gobind Sadan's programes are self-supporting. The staff and visiting volunteers live simply, creating a surplus far beyond their own needs which is used to provide services to those with disabilities and the poor.

Kirpal Sagar

If a 'Jesus place' at a Sikh ashram was unexpected, an invitation to the dedication of a building in which a church, a temple, a gurdwara and a mosque stood together was even more amazing. The invitation, which I received in 2007, was from Kirpal Sagar for an event to 'radiate a message of unity to the world.'

The creation of Kirpal Sagar was the work to which Dr Harbajan Singh devoted his life. Harbajan Singh was born in 1932 at Layalpur (now in Pakistan). After Partition, the family moved to Nag Kalan, where he practised as a doctor. The turning point came in 1961, when he met his master Sant Kirpal Singh.(xlvii)

Sant Kirpal Singh himself, who was born in 1894, even as a child, had unusual spiritual awareness. When his father once said to him, 'our friends will be your friends and our foes will be your foes.' Kirpal or 'Pal' as he was called by his Father, replied 'Father, your friends will be my friends, but it is not necessary that your foes be my foes, as your enmities may have been based on misunderstandings. Life is too short and I have not come to have enmities and hatreds. I have come to love all.' He also refused to eat meat. His father asked, 'Pal, why don't you take meat? It will do you good.' He replied, 'Is not meat dead flesh, and would you have me make a burial ground of my body?" The father smiled and the child had his own way. He was brought up to read the Sikh scriptures, but as he read more widely he came to see that all scriptures tell us there is a God.

After meeting with Kirpal Singh, Harbajan Singh became his disciple and his doctor. He was with Kirpal Singh when he died. He devoted his life to sharing his Master's message and his work as a doctor. On his last tour of the Punjab, in October 1973, Sant Kirpal Singh visited the Agriculture Farm located near Nawanshahr and laid the foundation stone of the hospital where Harbajan Singh worked.

Soon afterwards in 1974 Harbajan Singh started a movement called 'Unity of Man.' Two years later, with his wife Bibi Surinder Kaur came to the West. A little later a European Centre for 'Unity of Man' was set up at St Gilgen, near Salzburg. In 1993 the UN recognized the movement as an NGO.

In 1982, the foundation stone of Kirpal Sagar was laid. Kirpal means 'Grace', Sagar means 'Ocean' – thus the name Kirpal Sagar means 'Ocean of Grace'. Despite the political unrest in the Punjab at that time, Harbans Singh persisted with the project helped by his wife and volunteers from India and abroad. In 1994, an international conference was held there to mark the centenary of Sant Kirpal Singh. Harbajan Singh himself died in September 1995.

Kirpal Sagar is called 'a place for Man-making and Man-serving – based on Sant Kirpal Singh's motto 'Be good, Do good and Be one.' It is an amazing and beautiful campus with a charitable hospital, an Academy, with five hundred students, often from disadvantaged families, and a school for children. There is also a Library, a home for older people, accommodation for guests and a farm.

The very heart of Kirpal Sagar is the Sarova – a beautiful building, set in a lake, which is a place for silent reflection and meditation. On the roof there is a small church, a mosque, and a temple. They are symbols of unity and express the spirit of the building which is 'a place where the whole world can do their prayers.' It was particularly moving the following day to join a few others for a mass in the little church. As Surinder Kaur said, 'We have to know ourselves and to know the truth. We are soul, we are one and we are a drop of the Oversoul.'(xlviii)

Guru Nanak Nishkam Sewak Jatha

Another surprise came when I went to Kericho in Kenya to attend a conference of 'Globalisation for the Common Good,' arranged by my friend Kamran Mofid, with whom I had just co-authored a book called *Sustaining the Common Good*. There I discovered that the small town is home to Africa's largest Gurdwara. The conference was hosted by the Bhai Sahib Mohinder Singh, the head of Guru Nanak Nishkam Sewak Jatha (GNNSJ), whom I already knew. I had not realised the movement started in Kenya and was unaware of the major contribution that Sikhs made to the development of Uganda and Kenya.

Guru Nanak Niskham Sevak Jatha (GNNSJ) is a Sikh organisation, founded on the principles of selfless service to humanity (Niskham Sewa) of Sant Baba Puran Singh (1898-1983). It was set up by members of the Sikh community in Kericho. Baba Puran Singh was a Saint, but also a family man, who earned a living through honest toil and contributed selflessly to the welfare of those around him, irrespective of background.

Baba Puran Singh was born in 1898 in the Punjab village of Gurah in the Jallandar District. He was married at a young age. Although he spent many hours mediating and reading the Guru Granth Sahib, he always placed his duties as a householder at the forefront of his life.

Baba Puran Singh emmigrated to Kenya in 1916. He soon set up 'Kericho Wagon Works' in the small town and focused on earning a living, being a father to his family and helping others in the town. In 1952, his spirituality was given open recognition by a visiting saint, Sant Baba Mani Singh Ji, from India. Thereafter, his immense compassion and connection to God drew thousands to Kericho. His message was not just a philosophy of words; he was a personification of the proverb 'practice what you preach'.

He called for all religious service to be Nishkam – totally altruistic. In the 1970s, he came to England and soon decided to settle there. He travelled widely encouraging Sikhs to hold to their faith. He supported campaigns to allow Sikhs to wear the turban at their places of work.

Bhai Sahib Norang Singh (1926-1995), who had been identified by Puran Singh as his successor, was the second spiritual leader of the Nishkam Sewak Jatha. He was born in 1926 in the Punjab and spent some years at Amritsar before moving to Singapore. It was there that he met Baba Sohan Singh Ji and decided to live a life of hard work and devoted service to the Sangat. Bhai Sahib Norang Singh travelled to England and met Sant Baba Puran Singh Ji in 1968.

Bhai Sahib Norang Singh established the Birmingham Gurdwara, which was opened in 1977. Over the years and it has expanded and been embellished.

Bhai Sahib Norang Singh visited the Golden Temple in early 1994 and realized that repair of the Darbar Sahib was urgently needed. After exhaustive scrutiny and in recognition of its high ideals, it's strictly non-political nature and its excellent record of achievements, the Shiromani Gurdwara Prabandhak Committee, which was in charge of the Golden Temple, gave the sacred task of the re-gilding of the Golden Temple to Bhai Sahib and his movement in 1994. Much of the work was already completed before Bhai Sahib died in the summer of 1995. Before he died he entrusted the leadership of the movement to Bhai Sahib Bhai Mohinder Singh Ji.

Bhai Sahib Bhai Mohinder Singh was born in 1939. He spent most of his childhood in East Africa mainly in Kenya; with most of his secondary education in Nairobi. He then went to UK and qualified as a Civil and Structural Engineer. He undertook many large projects, working for a time with the National Housing Authority in Zambia.

In 1989, Mohinder Singh left Zambia and devoted his life to full time service under Bhai Sahib Norang Singh. Bhai Mohinder Singh moved the headquarters to Birmingham. The first main task was successfully to complete the UK Sangat's project of re-gilding the Sri Harimandir Sahib Sahib.(xlviiii)

He has also taken a lead in involving the Guru Nanak Nishkam Sewak Jatha in interfaith dialogue and has given generous support to many organisations. The memorable Langar, which it arranged at the Barcelona Parliament of World Religions, has already been mentioned. He has supported calls for a Charter of Forgiveness and the establishment of a Museum of Religions in Birmingham.

On Sunday, 22 April 2012 Dr Bhai Mohinder Singh was recognised for his "dedicated work to Roman Catholic-Sikh relations and for his enthusiastic commitment to working for peace among people of all faiths" and was made a Knight of the Pontifical Order of Pope St Gregory the Great, on Sunday 22 April 2012.

Sikhism's Message for the World

It is this commitment to peace and the universalism, inherent in the message of the Gurus, that makes it so important to learn more about Sikhism. The philosopher Bertrand Russell, Is reported to have said, 'If some lucky people survive the onslaught of the third world war of atomic and hydrogen bombs, then the Sikh religion will be the only means of guiding them.' When asked whether Sikhism is only capable of guiding humankind if there were a third world war, he replied, 'No, it has that capability, but the Sikhs have not brought out into the broad daylight the splendid doctrine of their religion which has come into existence for the benefit of the entire human race.'(l.)

Those mentioned above are shining examples of the many Sikhs who are sharing the message of the Gurus that all people are one and that it is only through devoted service in this world to those in need that one is at peace with God.

BIBLIOGRAPHY

Britsh Sikh Reports. http://www.britishsikhreport.org

Cole, Owen, *Sikhism*, London, Darton, Longman and Todd, 1982

Darshan Singh Tatla, *The Sikh Diaspora*, UCL Press, 1999.

Golden Temple, eds Parm Bakhshish Singh, Devinda Kumar Verma, R K Ghai and Gurshan Singh, Punjabi University, Patiala 1999.

Guru Guru Arjan Dev: Life, Martyrdom and Legacy, - papers of an international seminar, New Delhi 2006, ed by Mohinder Singh, (National Institute of Panjab Studies, New Delhi), and Prithiipal Singh Kapur, (Pro-Vice Chancellor, Guru Nanak University, Amritsar)

Harbans Singh, *The Heritage of the Sikhs*, New Delhi, 1983

Cunningham, J D, *History of the Sikhs*, (1849), Reprint by Rupa Publications, New Delhi, 2002

Encylopaedia of Sikhism, Ed Harbans Singh, Patiala, Punjabi University, 4 vols, 1992

Eternal Guru: Granth Sahib, ed Mohinder Singh, Guru Nanak Nishkam Sewak Jatha, Birmingham, 2008

Khalsa Consensus Translation, www global grey.co.uk, 2013 Gopal Singh 1960

Khushwant Singh, *Hymns of The Gurus*, Penguin Books Ltd and Kindle, n.d.

Macauliffe, M.A. *The Sikh Religion*. 6 vols, Oxford University Press, 1909.

McLeod,W.H, *Sikhs and Sikhism*, [one volume including ' Guru Nanak and the Sikh Religion' (1968), Early Sikh Traditions'(1980),'The Evolution   of the Sikh Community,'(1976) and 'Who is a Sikh?' (1989)] Oxford University Press, 1999

Patwant Singh, *The Sikhs*, London, John Murray, 1999

Perspectives on Guru Nanak, ed Harbans Singh - papers of an international seminar held in 1969, Patiala, the Punjabi University, 1975

Sikhism, papers by Fauja Singh, Trilochan Singh, Gurbachan Singh Talib, J P Singh Uberoi, and Sohan Singh, Patiala, Punjabi University, 1969.

Sohinder Singh Sachdev, *Story of the Sikhs*, ISBN 9781475275971 – no other details

Sri Guru Granth Sahib: trans by Gurbachan Singh Talib in his Introduction to the Sri Guru Granth Sahib, Punjabi University, Patiala, 1997 4 vols [I have usually quoted from this translation but have also used other translations]

Studies in Sikh Philosophy and Culture, Ed, Jaswinder Kaur Dhillon, Amritsar, Guru Nanak University, 2004.

Sikhism

Studies on Guru Granth Sahib , Ed, Balwant Singh Dhillon, , Amritsar, Guru Nanak University, 2004.
South Indian Studies on Sikhism, Ed, N. Muthu Mohan Amritsar, Guru Nanak University, 2004.

The are many Sikh journals, magazines and news-letters,and web-sites. Journals such as *The Sikh Messenger, Studies in Sikhism and Comparative Religion* and *Journal of Sikh Studies* are also important sources of information

NOTES

i Singh, Khushwant. *Hymns Of The Gurus* (Kindle Locations 1825-1830). Penguin Books Ltd. Kindle Edition.

ii Sirdar Kapur Singh, *Guru Guru Arjan Dev: Life, Martyrdom and Legacy*, Proceedings of an International Seminar in 2006, Guru Nanak Dev University, Amritsar p.74

iii P.S. Kapur, ibid, p.95, see also p. 49

iv *Varan Bhai Gurdas* 26, 24

v Quoted by Patwant Singh, *The Sikhs*, London, John Murray, 1999 p. 49 from J.D Cunningham

vi J S Grewal 'The Khalsa of Guru Gobind Singh' in *From Guru Nanak to Maharaja Ranjit Sing,* 29.

vii Quoted by Own Cole, *The Gurus in Sikhism,* p. 28. He suggests there is some doubt about the accuracy of the tradition.

viii The instructions about faith and behaviour are knowns as *rahitnamas*

ix Quoted by W H McLeod, *Who is a* Sikh? From Ratan Singh Bhangu, *Prachin Panth Prakas*, 16, 32-6 (p. 27)

x *Golden Temple*, eds Parm Bakhshish Singh, Devinda Kumar Verma, R K Ghai and Gurshan Singh, Punjabi University, Patiala 1999, p. 623

xi Harbans Singh, *The Heritage of the Si*khs, New Delhi, 1983, p.47

xii Golden Temple p. 78

xiii Quoted by Gurbachan Singh Talib in his Introduction to the Sri Guru Granth Sahib, Patiala, Punjabi University, 1997, p Quoted in *Guru Arjan Dev: Life, Martyrdom and Legacy*, p.69

xiv Owen Cole, *Sikhism*, London, Darton, Longman and Todd, 1982, pp. 55-6

xv Patwant Singh, p. 81 quoting from William Irvine, *Political History of the Sikhs*.

xvi J D Cunningham, *History of the Sikhs,*(1849), reprint by RupaPublications, New Delhi, 2002

xvii See a detailed account http://www.searchsikhism.com/baba-banda-singh

xviii Information about Cunningham is from Patwant Singh's Foreword. p 115 Quoted by Patwan Singh, p.141

       xviii *Ibid* p 145

xix *Ibid* p. 137 quoting Kapur Singh

xx *Sikh Rahit Maryada*, Shiromani Gurdwara Parbandhak Committee (SGPC) 1950.,

p. 8 See also Mcleod last section, p.96

xxi   Burns, John F. (15 October 1997). "In India, Queen Bows Her Head Over a Massacre in 1919". New York Times.

xxii   Ibid

xxiii   David   Cameron marks   British   1919   Amritsar Massacre".News. BBC. 20 February 2013.

xxiv   https://tribune.com.pk/story/619750/agony-of- women-during- partition/

xxv Patwant Singh, p 228

xxxi http://www.punjabdata.com/Sikh- Population-In-India.

xxxii http://www.worldatlas.com/articles/countries-with- the-largest-sikhpopulations.htm1

xxxiii   www.ccss.org/Resources/Documents/Sikh Migration to
CA. Much of the material is based on the
researches of Margaret Hill.

xxxiv My Readers Digest Universal Dictionary says of the Caucasoid ethnic group that it pertains to 'peoples indigenous to or inhabiting Europe, North Africa, Southwestern Asia and the Indian subcontinent and persons of this ancestry in other parts of the world.'

xxxv http://time.com/4569129/racist-anti-semitic-incidents-donald-trump/

xxxvi The *Eternal Guru Granth Sahib* ,ed Mohinder Singh, Guru Nanak Nishkam Sewak Jatha, Birmingham, 2008 p. 53

xxxviii Quoted by Trilochan Singh in Sikhism, p. 41.

xxxvii, Ibid, p.3

xxxviii http://www.sikhiwiki.org/index.php/Bhai_Kanhaiya xxxix
http://indiatoday.intoday.in/story/sikh-man-harman-singh-felicitated- removed-turban-help-child- newzealand/1/448928.html: and http://www.mid-day.com/articles/new- zealand-sikh-who-removed-turban-to-help-wounded-boy-lauded-worldwide/16219175

xl www.patheos.com/blogs/friendlyatheist /2016/06/07/its-this-drowning-dogs-lucky-day-when-a- sikh-samaritan-disobeys-his- religion

xli G.S Puri 'Nature Consciousness in the Sikh Faith.' In   *Studies in Sikhism and Comparative Religion,* Guru Nanak Foundation, New Delhi, Vol VIII, No 1, pp 91-101

xlii *www.sikhanswers.com/rehat-maryada-code-of.../sikh-attitude-to-inter-faith-marriages/*

xliii *www.bbc.co.uk/news/uk-34043575*

xliv www.sikhanswers.com/modern-youth-issues/sikh-attitude-to-homosexuality.
xlvi www.allaboutsikhs.com/sikh-ceremonies/funeral-ceremonies-antam-sanskar
xlvii http://www.gobindsadan.org/
xlviii http://www.sant-kirpal-singh.org
xlviiiii Quoted in the book recording the World Conference on Unity of Man in December 2007, held to mark the 75th Birth Anniversary of Dr Harbajan Singh
xlviiii Guru Nanak Nishkam Sewak Jatha 18- 20 Soho road
Handsworth, Birmingham b21 See also www.sikhiwiki.org/index.php/_ Guru Nanak_Nishkam_Sewak_Jatha
l. Quoted in *The Eternal Guru Granth Sahib*, p..16

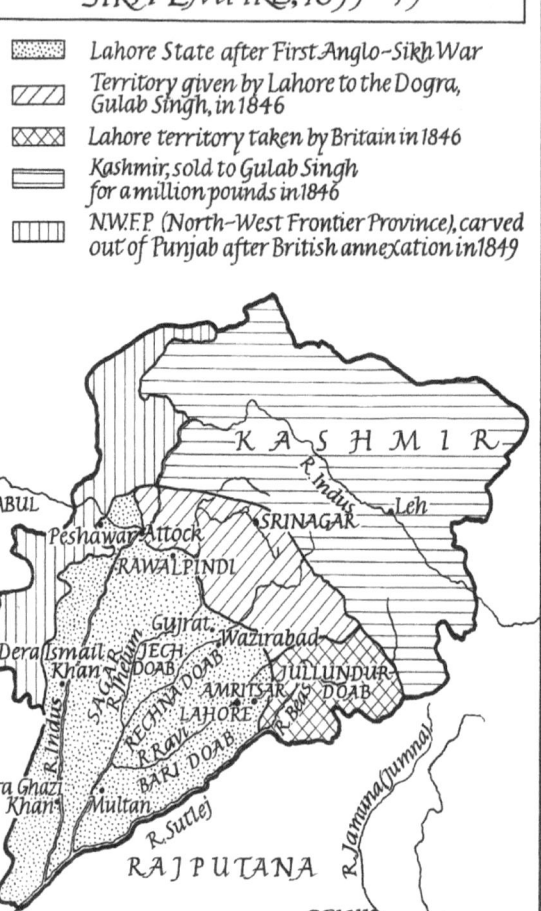

3. THE DISMANTLING OF THE SIKH EMPIRE, 1839–49

- Lahore State after First Anglo-Sikh War
- Territory given by Lahore to the Dogra, Gulab Singh, in 1846
- Lahore territory taken by Britain in 1846
- Kashmir, sold to Gulab Singh for a million pounds in 1846
- N.W.F.P. (North-West Frontier Province), carved out of Punjab after British annexation in 1849

KABUL

KASHMIR

R. Indus

SRINAGAR

Leh

Peshawar Attock

RAWALPINDI

Gujrat

Dera Ismail Khan

JECH DOAB

Wazirabad

SAGAR DOAB

R. Jhelum

RECHNA DOAB

AMRITSAR

JULLUNDUR DOAB

LAHORE

R. Chenab

R. Ravi

R. Beas

BARI DOAB

Dera Ghazi Khan

Multan

R. Indus

R. Sutlej

RAJPUTANA

R. Jamuna (Jumna)

DELHI

R. Ganges

miles 0 100 200

Other books by Marcus Braybrooke

Bridge of Stars: 365 Prayers, Blessings and Meditations from Around the World 978-1903296271

Widening Vision. A History of the World Congress of Faiths and the Growing Interfaith Movement.
978-1291362329

Beacons of Light: 100 Holy People who have shaped The history of humanity. 978-1-84694-185-6

Christianity; An Explorer's Guide. 978-1-291-55714-5

*Peace in Our Hearts: Peace in Our World –
a mediation for every day.* 978-1-326-31527-6

1000 World Prayers (editor)   978-1-1903-816-172

A Heart for the World: A Program to Transform the World Based on Non-violence and Compassion
978-1291355277

Islam: a Christian Approach. 978-1291355277
Hinduism; a Christian Approach
Some books are available as e-books